Four Seasons in Flannel

JEAN WELLS & LAWRY THORN

23 PROJECTS—QUILTS & MORE

C&T PUBLISHING

© 2002 Jean Wells and Lawry Thorn

Editor-in-Chief: Darra Williamson

Editor: Candie Frankel

Technical Editors: Candie Frankel, Gael Betts

Copyeditor/Proofreader: Kathryn Pellman

Photography: Valori Wells

Cover Designer: Christina D. Jarumay

Design Director/Book Designer: Christina D. Jarumay

Illustrator: Tim Manibusan

Production Assistant: Jeffrey Carrillo

Editorial Assistant: Stacy Chamness

Published by C&T Publishing, Inc., P.O. Box 1456, Lafayette, California 94549

Library of Congress Cataloging-in-Publication Data

Wells, Jean.
  Four seasons in flannel : 23 projects--quilts & more / Jean Wells and Lawry Thorn.
      p. cm.
  Includes bibliographical references and index.
  ISBN 1-57120-178-5
  1. Patchwork--Patterns. 2. Quilting. 3. Flannel. I. Thorn, Lawry. II. Title.
  TT835 .W4652 2002
  746.46'041--dc21

                    2002002064

Printed in China
10 9 8 7 6 5 4 3 2 1

Acknowledgments

A very grateful thank-you to our special stitchers: Victoria Brady, Barbara Ferguson, Debbie Kohler, Gerri Moore, Sherry Morris, Patricia Raymond, Jacki Richards, Ursula Searles, Laura Simmons, Valori Wells, and Pat Welsh. Some did embroidery, others did buttonhole stitch appliqué, and Patricia machine-quilted most of the quilts.

A very special thank-you to Valori Wells, daughter and coworker, for photographing all of the quilts and projects.

Introduction...6

The Basics...7

TABLE OF

Spring...25

Summer...46

Fall...72

CONTENTS

Winter...103

Introduction

Four Seasons in Flannel is a project book for quilters and others who enjoy making their own decorative home accents and gifts. If you've never stitched with flannel fabrics before, you're in for a treat. Flannel is soft, cuddly, and easy to work with. It needles beautifully by hand or machine, giving quilters of all skill levels and abilities a satisfying sewing experience. We also introduce a similar material, wool felt, and show how it, too, can be appliquéd and embroidered.

The tall pine forests surrounding our hometown of Sisters, Oregon, inspired our embroidery designs and buttonhole stitch appliqués. Woodland animals, chickadees, even fish turn up on our quilts. For each season—spring, summer, fall, and winter—we developed a theme quilt in a unique color palette.

All of the quilts are designed around thirteen different pieced blocks and units. Illustrated instructions for piecing the blocks and working various embroidery stitches are presented in the opening chapter. Should you choose to combine these different embroidery, appliqué, and block designs on your own, your project options will multiply far beyond the nine quilts and fourteen accessory projects we feature here.

Flannel is not just for cold, wintry climates or thick, warm quilts. With a lighter palette and a wide selection of project ideas, flannel makes the perfect quilter's companion, no matter where you live. Let Four Seasons in Flannel show you the way.

Jean and Lawry

THE BASICS

If you're like us, you can hardly wait to start planning your next quilt or project. Before you jump in, read this chapter. It will help you become better acquainted with the flannel and wool felt fabrics you'll be using, the ins and outs of buttonhole stitch appliqué, and techniques for hand embroidery. Directions for making basic patchwork blocks and finishing your quilts and pillows are given, too.

Working with Flannel Fabric

Flannel is a woven cotton or wool textile with a soft, brushed surface. The cozy softness invites you to touch the fabric and cuddle up with it. To create this soft, pliable texture, manufacturers use a mechanical finishing process, called "napping," that raises the fiber ends. When you examine the flannels at your favorite quilt shop, you'll probably notice differences in the amount of napping and softness, depending on where the flannel was milled. Higher-quality flannels have a soft, thick nap, while lesser-quality flannels feel thin and flimsy in comparison. If you'd like to learn more about how flannel fabric is produced, we recommend *From Fiber to Fabric* by Harriet Hargrave.

You can safely combine different weights of flannel in a single project as long as you preshrink your selections first. It is not absolutely necessary to preshrink high-quality flannels, especially if you want to create a washed-quilt look using cotton batting, but for most flannels, preshrinking is a good idea.

> **QUILTER'S TIP**
>
> Flannels have a fairly open weave and tend to shrink more than ordinary cottons. We have found that the average flannel fabric shrinks from $1/2$" to 1" per yard in length and up to $1/2$" in width.

The materials listed for our projects allow enough 44"-wide yardage for you to preshrink the flannels once. First, zigzag or serge the cut edges to prevent fraying. Wash the flannels in the sink (good for small cuts) or on a gentle cycle in the washer, and then put the fabric in the dryer on a low-heat setting. Some flannels will require touch-up pressing and others won't.

Flannel is ideal for the simple pieced blocks and borders we've used in our designs. The raised nap causes the patchwork pieces to stick together during stitching. In fact, the only times you'll need to use pins is with thinner flannels or on long seams to prevent stretching. Be sure to use an accurate $1/4$" seam allowance. If you are using a lesser-quality, "stretchy" flannel, you may want to adjust your cutting dimensions to allow for $1/2$" seams. After sewing, press each seam gently by setting the iron on it and holding for a few seconds. Avoid ironing back and forth, which can cause stretching.

You can quilt flannel by hand or machine—the fabric is so soft and needles so easily, it is a joy to do either. The surface nap helps show off the quilting lines. We like to stitch close to the seams to minimize the stress placed on them and to keep each seam in place. Echo quilting and designs that relate to the quilt overall work well within larger areas.

One more word of advice: Today's flannels are sold in many exciting colors and novelty designs. They tend to come and go quickly in the marketplace, so if you see something you like, don't delay in making your purchase.

Working with Wool Felt

Wool felt is a fun fabric to use. Like the felt you remember from childhood, it's slightly thick and the cut edges don't need finishing. The soft fibers are easy to needle, making it perfect for buttonhole stitch embroidery. You've probably seen wool felt used for penny rugs, Santa and doll clothes, purses, wall hangings, and similar projects.

Most wool felts sold today are not 100 percent wool but blends of wool and rayon. The felts we used in our projects have wool/rayon blends of 20/80 and 35/65, but 50/50 and 70/30

blends are also available. Wool felt is manufactured at 36" wide and 72" wide. Depending on where you shop, you can buy it off the bolt by the yard or in smaller precut pieces. As you will see from our projects, the colors are rich and sometimes heathery—much more subtle and sophisticated than the bright primary colors generally associated with felt.

We like to pretreat wool felt to make it even softer than it already is and to give the surface a slightly nubby texture. Fill a basin or sink with hot water. Immerse the felt in the water and let it soak for a few minutes. Then lift it out and squeeze gently, removing as much water as possible. Place the felt in the dryer along with an old clean towel, and run the dryer at a low-heat setting. The towel will help absorb the excess moisture, dye, and lint. When the felt is nearly dry, remove it from the dryer and lay it flat on a fresh towel to finish drying. The shrinkage with this method is approximately three to five inches in both directions. To avoid further shrinkage, dry-clean projects made from wool felt.

Buttonhole Stitch Appliqué

Fusible appliqués with buttonhole stitching around the edges appear in projects throughout the book. Needles glide easily through flannel and wool felt, making this decorative stitchery surprisingly easy to do. Here's what you'll need:

✛ **Paper-Backed Fusible Web**. Paper-backed fusible web is composed of a thin piece of paper with a web or dots of adhesive on one side. The adhesive, identifiable by its rough texture, is activated by the heat of an iron applied to the smooth paper side. Fusible web is used to join two pieces of fabric together, such as an appliqué to a quilt block, without sewing. For buttonhole stitch appliqué, look for a product that is "sewable," that is, one that allows a needle to pass through easily. Some adhesives are simply too heavy or too thick for comfortable stitching. Read the label carefully when you purchase the fusible web, and store it rolled, not folded, to prevent the adhesive from pulling away from the paper. The manufacturer's instructions will tell you more about using this time-saving product.

✛ **Scissors.** You'll need two pairs of scissors: one pair for cutting the paper-backed fusible web and paper patterns and another small, sharp pair for cutting out fabric appliqués and snipping embroidery threads.

✛ **Needles.** To work buttonhole stitch, use a size 8 or size 10 embroidery needle. The eye of the needle must be large enough for the thread to pass through, and the needle point needs to be sharp. Keep extras on hand and change to a fresh needle when the point becomes dulled.

✛ **Thread.** Two strands of six-strand embroidery floss are most commonly used for buttonhole stitch appliqué. You can use a single color, such as black, to embroider around all the appliqués in a project, or you can change the floss color with each new appliqué shape. DMC size 8 perle cotton, a twisted thread with a slight sheen, can also be used and is especially effective on wool felt projects.

Fusible Appliqués

Here's how to make and apply fusible appliqués, step by step:

1. Place the paper-backed fusible web on the pattern, paper side up, and trace the pattern outline with a pencil. Note that unless the pattern is symmetrical, the image appears backwards. It will reverse itself in the fusing process.

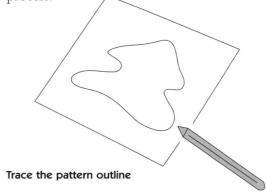

Trace the pattern outline

2. Cut around the traced motif with paper scissors, about ¼" beyond the pencil line.

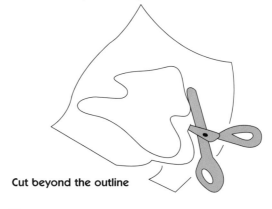

Cut beyond the outline

3. Place the rough, adhesive side of the cutout on the wrong side of the fabric you have chosen for the appliqué. Follow the manufacturer's instructions to fuse the cutout to the fabric. Do not let the pieces overheat! If the iron is too hot, the adhesive may melt through the fabric and discolor it.

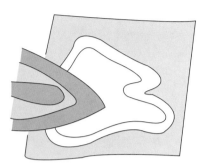

Fuse the shape to the fabric

4. Use fabric scissors to cut out the appliqué directly on the pencil line. Remove the paper backing, using a pin to loosen it if necessary. Repeat steps 1–4 for each appliqué.

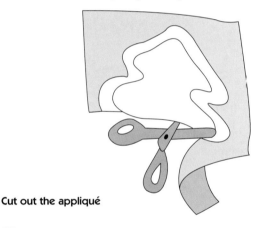

Cut out the appliqué

5. Position the appliqués on the background fabric, right sides facing up. When you are satisfied with the placement, fuse each appliqué to the background fabric using an up-and-down motion with the iron. If the appliqués overlap, work from the background to the foreground.

Overlapping Appliqués

QUILTER'S TIP

Fuse on a flat, hard surface protected by a towel. Use a work table—not your good dining room table—because the heat of the iron may cause the towel to stick to the tabletop.

Buttonhole Stitch

After the flannel appliqués are fused in place, embellish the edges with buttonhole stitch, or blanket stitch, as it is sometimes called. This stitch can also be used as a decorative edging and to hold down wool felt appliqués that are not prefused. Use two strands of floss in a size 8 or size 10 embroidery needle (or sharps).

To embroider the basic stitch, hold the work with the edge of the appliqué toward you. Draw the needle out through the background fabric, just below the edge of the appliqué. Hold down the thread with your left thumb. Insert the needle into the appliqué at A and come back out through the background fabric at B. Pull the needle through and over the working thread to form the first stitch. Continue in this way, working the stitches from left to right, to form a neat finish on the edge of the appliqué. Space the stitches $1/8$" to $1/4$" apart.

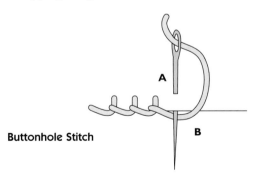

Buttonhole Stitch

To stitch around a corner or point, work all the way to the corner, drawing the needle out at B. Reinsert the needle in the background fabric a few threads away to anchor the floss at B. Reemerge a couple of fabric threads over at C and resume stitching.

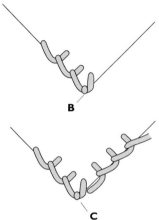

Stitching a Corner

On an inside point, plan your stitches so that they are an equal distance apart and flow evenly. When the appliqué curves out, bring the "legs" of the stitches closer together; when the appliqué curves in, let the legs flare out.

Stitching Curved Edges

QUILTER'S TIP

Simulate a hand-worked buttonhole stitch using your sewing machine. Consult your machine manual to find the correct setting. Use heavier thread, such as Jeans Stitch by YLI, and a larger needle. Practice on scrap fabric before stitching your project.

More Embroidery Stitches

Appliqués aren't the only way to add fun motifs and contrasting textures to your projects. We used stem stitch, backstitch, and French knots to embroider pine boughs, chickadees, bunnies, and other designs on our background fabrics. Herringbone stitch and featherstitch are perfect for embellishing crazy-patch seams.

To work these stitches, use two strands of floss in a size 8 or size 10 embroidery needle (sharps can also be used), just as for buttonhole stitch. If you like to hold the fabric taut in an embroidery hoop for stitching, allow for extra fabric in your purchase, cut the background fabric a little larger than specified in the project cutting directions, and trim to size after the embroidery is completed. Another option is to work the embroidery after a quilt is partially assembled, as we did for *Lakeside* (page 47).

Embroidery Design Transfer

Begin by tracing the design on a good-quality tracing paper, strong enough to take pressing with an iron but light enough to see through. Turn the tracing wrong side up, and go over the design lines with a Sulky iron-on transfer pen. To complete the transfer, turn the tracing wrong side down on the background fabric and press with a hot iron. (Consult the pen manufacturer's directions for the full details.) We suggest testing the pen on a small sample of the background fabric to make sure the lines can be removed later in case the embroidery threads do not completely cover them.

Stem Stitch

Come out at A. Hold down the thread with your left thumb, go in at B, and come out at C. Pull through to complete the stitch. Continue in this way, moving from left to right along the marked design line. The stitches should overlap slightly to create a dense line.

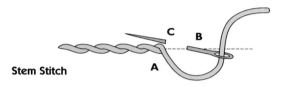

Stem Stitch

Backstitch

Use a backstitch for outlining. Come out at A. Insert the needle at B and come out at C. Pull through to set the first stitch. Continue in this way, working from right to left. Make all the stitches the same length.

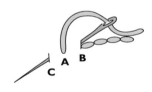

Backstitch

French Knot

Use this stitch for animal eyes or when a design calls for small dots. Practice on scrap fabric first. Come out at A, or the spot where the stitch will be formed. Holding the needle with the right hand and the floss with the left hand, wrap the floss around the needle two or three times. Still holding the floss taut, insert the needle back into the fabric a few threads away from A. With the floss snug but not tight around the needle, slowly draw the needle through to the wrong side of the fabric to set the French knot. Secure with a small knot on the wrong side.

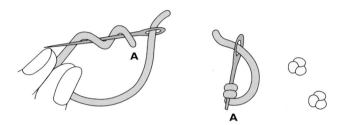

French Knot

Herringbone Stitch

Work this stitch along the edge of a seam or straddling a seam. Come out at A. Insert the needle at B and come out at C. Pull through, creating a diagonal stitch. Insert the needle at D and come out at E. Pull through, creating a second diagonal stitch that crosses over the first one. Continue in this way, moving from left to right, so that each stitch crosses over the previous one.

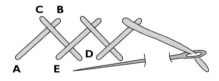

Herringbone Stitch

Featherstitch

Work this lacy stitch over a seam. Come out at A. Hold down the thread with your left thumb. Insert the needle at B and come out at C. Pull the needle through the fabric and over the working thread to anchor the first stitch. Insert the needle at D and come out at E, drawing through to anchor the second stitch. Continue back and forth, stitching toward yourself.

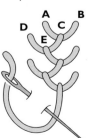

Featherstitch

Patchwork Blocks and Units

This section contains piecing instructions for thirteen blocks and units. Follow the individual project instructions to cut your fabric pieces and assemble the quilt tops. You might be inspired to combine the blocks and units into your own quilt designs.

Four-Patch

Four-Patch features four squares sewn together to make a larger square. If two fabrics are used, the squares form a checkerboard look. Use the strip piecing method shown here to speed up the sewing when you need multiple blocks.

1. Place two strips of fabric right sides together. Stitch together along one long edge with a ¼" seam allowance. Press the seam allowance toward the darker fabric.

2. Cut the strip into segments equal to the width of a single cut strip.

cut

3. Sew two segments together as shown, matching the seam lines.

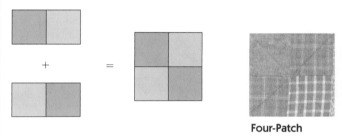

+ =

Four-Patch

Checkerboard Strips

Follow the Four-Patch instructions, steps 1 and 2. Stitch the segments together to make a strip of the required grid size.

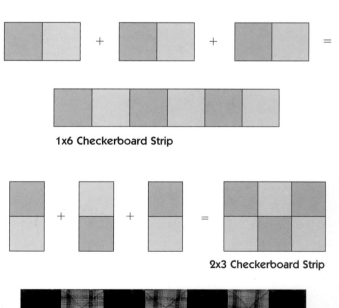

+ + =

1x6 Checkerboard Strip

+ + =

2x3 Checkerboard Strip

Double Four-Patch

Double Four-Patch uses two Four-Patches and two plain squares. The completed block is also a Four-Patch.

1. Cut a square the same size as the Four-Patch. Stitch a square and a Four-Patch together. Repeat.

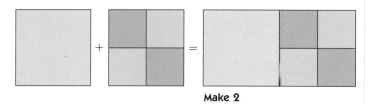

Make 2

2. Join the two units together.

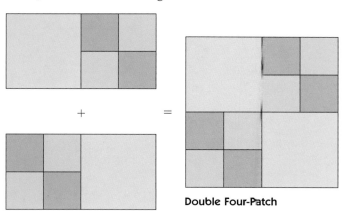

Double Four-Patch

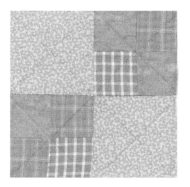

Nine-Patch

Start with nine equal-size squares. For a checkerboard look, cut five of the squares from one fabric and four of the squares from a contrasting fabric.

1. Arrange the nine squares in three rows as shown. Stitch the squares in each row together. Press toward the darker square.

2. Join row 1 to row 2. Then join row 3 to row 2. Press toward the block's outer edge.

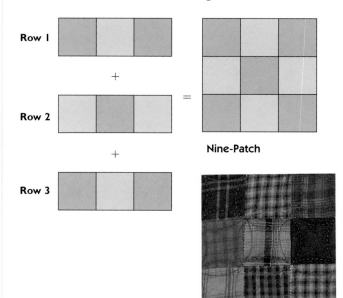

Row I

+

Row 2

+

Row 3

Nine-Patch

Pine Bough Logs

The center of this block is constructed in rows like a Nine-Patch, using five squares and four rectangles. More strips and squares are added as a border. If you are making multiple blocks, the basic units can be strip-pieced.

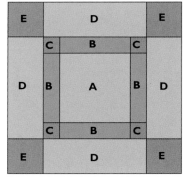

Block Diagram

1. Stitch two B's to opposite edges of A, right sides together, using a ¼" seam allowance. Press toward the darker fabric. In the same way, stitch two C's to each remaining B. Press in the opposite direction, so the seams will butt when the pieced units are joined.

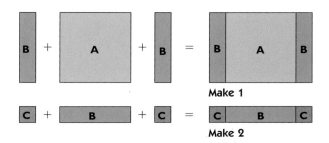

2. Arrange the pieced units in three rows as shown. Join row 1 to row 2. Then join row 3 to row 2. Press toward the block's outer edge. This completes the center of the block.

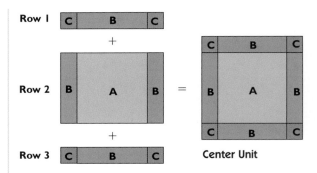

3. Stitch two E's to opposite edges of D. Press. Repeat.

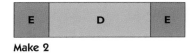

Make 2

4. Stitch two D's to opposite edges of the center unit. Press. Arrange the pieced units in three rows. Join the rows together.

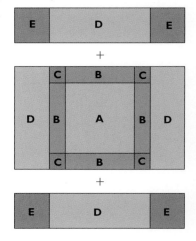

Embroidery adds the finishing touch to this Pine Bough Logs block:

Pathways

Pathways is constructed in three rows like a Nine-Patch block, but it has more variation. The pieces include rectangles as well as squares and the row heights don't have to match.

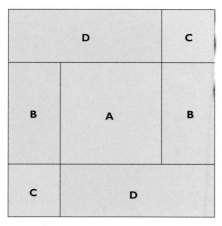

Block Diagram

1. Stitch two B's to opposite edges of A, right sides together, using a ¼" seam allowance. Press toward the darker fabric.

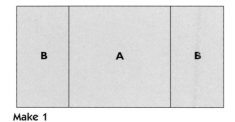

Make 1

2. Stitch C to D. Press. Repeat.

Make 2

3. Arrange the pieced units in three rows as shown. Join row 1 to row 2. Then join row 3 to row 2. Press toward the block's outer edge.

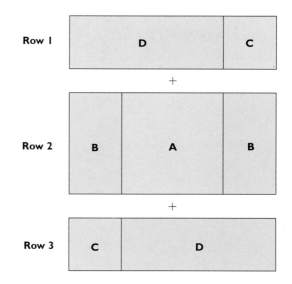

A completed Pathways block:

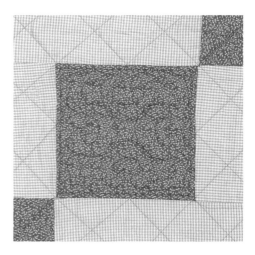

Half-Square & Double Half-Square Triangles

Half-square triangles are made by cutting squares in half on the diagonal. The half-square triangle pieced unit is a square with a diagonal seam.

1. Place two half-square triangles right sides together. Stitch along the diagonal edge with a $1/4$" seam allowance. If you are making multiple units, feed each pair through the machine in a continuous chain, without cutting the thread.

2. Clip the chain-pieced units apart. Lay each unit on a pressing surface with the darker triangle on top. Fold back the top triangle and press from the right side, so the seam falls under the darker fabric. Trim off the nubs to even up the square.

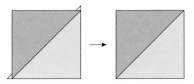

Half-Square Triangle Unit

The double half-square triangle pieced unit is a rectangle with two diagonal seams.

1. Start with a rectangle and two squares. Fold one square in half diagonally, press to set the fold, and open. Align the square on the rectangle, right sides together. Stitch on the diagonal fold line through both layers.

2. Trim $1/4$" beyond the stitching line.

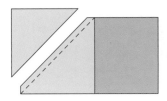

3. Fold back the triangular piece over the seam allowance. Press from the right side.

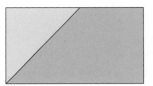

4. Repeat steps 1 and 2 with the remaining square.

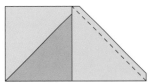

5. Fold back and press the second triangle to complete the unit.

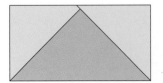

Double Half-Square Triangle Unit

Flying Geese

Stitch several double half-square triangle units together to make the Flying Geese pattern. Make sure all the points face in the same direction.

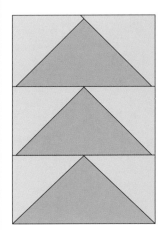

Flying Geese

Friendship Star

The Friendship Star is made with half-square triangles. This version uses a Four-Patch block in the center.

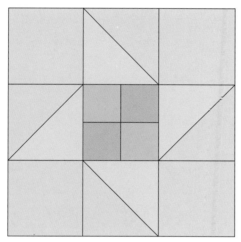

Block Diagram

1. Make one Four-Patch block (page 14). Make four half-square triangle units (page 18) and cut four plain squares, all the same size as the Four-Patch.

Make 1

Make 4

Cut 4

2. Arrange the nine squares in three rows as shown. Stitch together and press. Join row 1 to row 2. Then join row 3 to row 2. Press toward the block's outer edge.

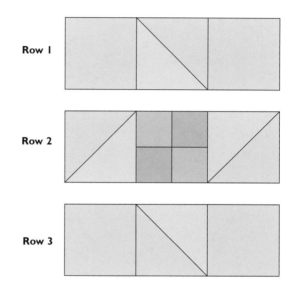

Row 1

Row 2

Row 3

A completed Friendship Star block:

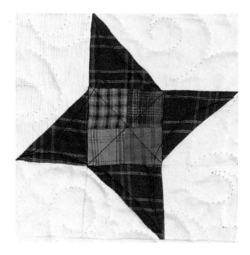

Animal Tracks

Use half-square triangles and squares to frame the center square of this block.

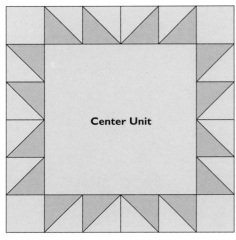

Block Diagram

1. Make 16 half-square triangle units (page 18). Cut four plain squares the same size.

Make 16 **Cut 4**

2. Arrange four half-square triangle units side by side as shown. Stitch them together. Repeat to make four strips total. Add a plain square to each end of two of the strips. Press toward the darker fabric.

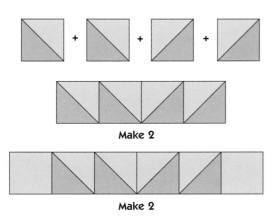

Make 2

Make 2

3. Join the shorter strips to the side edges of the square center unit, making sure that the points face out. Join the longer strips to the top and bottom edges.

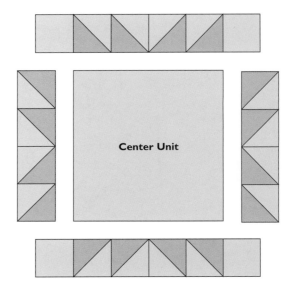

A completed Animal Tracks block:

Pine Star

This star appears to be a Sawtooth, but it is pieced on the diagonal. Templates are used to cut some of the pieces.

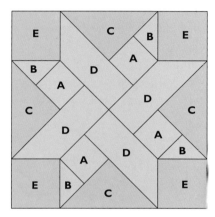

Block Diagram

1. Stitch B to A, right sides together, using a $\frac{1}{4}$" seam allowance. Press toward the darker fabric.

2. Stitch C to AB. Press.

3. Stitch D to ABC. Press.

4. Begin the Y-seam construction by placing an E square on the BC corner of a pieced unit, right sides together and raw edges aligned. Stitch E to B in the direction of the arrow, starting at the outside edge and stopping $\frac{1}{4}$" from the opposite edge of the square. Open out the fabric, but do not press. Make four ABCDE units.

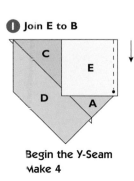

1 Join E to B

Begin the Y-Seam
Make 4

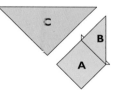

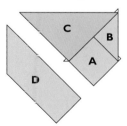

5. To complete the Y-seam and join two units together, stitch two more seams in the order shown. For each seam, start at the outer edge and stitch in toward the middle, stopping $\frac{1}{4}$" before the edge (the dot on D). Press the seam allowance in the direction it wants to go. Repeat to join the two remaining units.

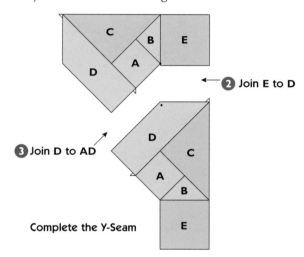

2 Join E to D

3 Join D to AD

Complete the Y-Seam

6. Join the two halves to complete the block. Press.

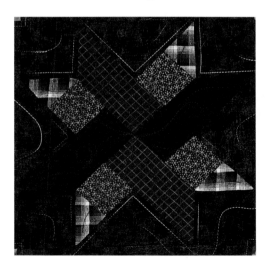

Pine Tree

Templates are used to cut all or most of the pieces in this block.

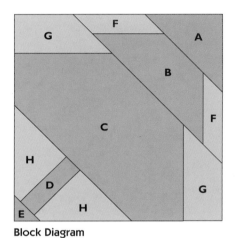

Block Diagram

1. Stitch two F's to the shorter edges of B, right sides together, using a ¼" seam allowance. Press toward the tree.

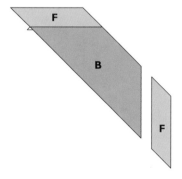

2. Stitch two G's to C. Press toward the tree.

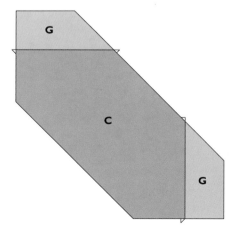

3. Stitch two H's to D. Press toward the tree trunk.

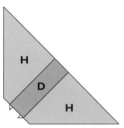

4. Join the three pieced units as shown. Add triangles A and E at each end to complete the block. Press all the seams in one direction.

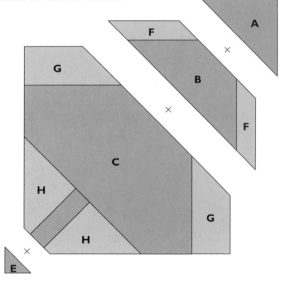

The finished block can be set square as shown or on point so the tree stands upright.

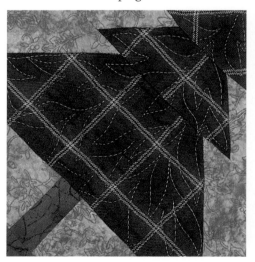

Finishing a Quilt

To finish a quilt, you need to prepare the backing, assemble and quilt the layers, and bind the edges.

The Backing

The backing for a quilt must be at least 2" larger than the quilt top on each side. For example, if your quilt top measures 36" x 48", you'll need a backing that measures at least 40" x 52". For a large backing, you may have to join several pieces of fabric together. To avoid a seam down the middle, cut the backing fabric in half on the crosswise grain, cut one of the pieces in half on the lengthwise grain, and join together as shown. Press the seams open.

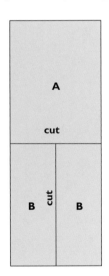
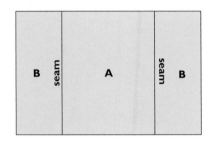

Layering

Place the backing on a hard flat surface, wrong side up. Tape down each edge at the middle, keeping the fabric taut. Tape out to each corner, continuing to keep the fabric taut. Lay the batting on top of the backing and pat out any wrinkles. Center the quilt top on the batting, right side up. Make sure the quilt top looks straight on each side. You can always pat a little extra fullness toward the interior of the quilt top.

We recommend basting with safety pins, particularly for machine quilting. Start at the center of the quilt and insert a pin every three to four inches, working out to the edges. Continue until the entire quilt sandwich is pinned.

Quilting

Flannel quilts can be quilted by hand or machine, depending on the effect you want. Look to the quilt itself for shapes or motifs that you can repeat or echo in the open spaces of the quilt. When a design theme is repeated in this way, the quilt gains unity and coherence. A design picked at random, with no relationship to the overall theme of the quilt, will appear like an afterthought. Work the quilting lines approximately three to four inches apart across the surface. Try to keep the spacing between the quilting lines relatively even. Quilting that is evenly distributed will be more pleasing to the eye.

Binding

There are numerous ways to bind a quilt, and each quilter seems to find her favorite method. The single-fold binding described here accommodates the extra thickness of flannel.

1. Cut a binding strip 1½" wide and 1" longer than one side edge of the quilt, piecing the strips end to end to obtain the needed length.

2. Place the strip on the quilt top, right sides together and raw edges aligned, so that the binding extends ½" beyond the quilt top at each end. Use a walking foot to stitch ¼" from the raw edges through all layers. Trim off the excess batting and backing fabric to match the ¼" seam allowance.

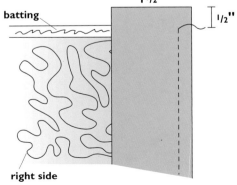

3. Press the long raw edge of the binding strip ¼" to the wrong side. Fold the binding onto the back of the quilt, line up the pressed fold on the stitching line, and pin every few inches. Slip-stitch the binding to the quilt, folding in the excess at each end. The thickness of the batting and flannel should fill out the binding.

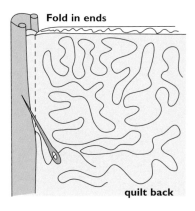

4. Repeat steps 1–3 to bind the opposite edge of the quilt. Then bind the remaining two edges. The binding will overlap at the corners.

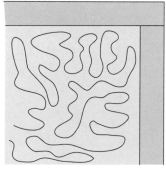

A Bound Corner

Finishing a Pillow

A pillow can be stuffed with loose fiberfill or with a pillow form. One advantage to using a pillow form is that it can be easily removed to launder the pillow cover. Sewing the back of a square pillow cover with two overlapping pieces of fabric is one way to create the necessary opening. Cut the pieces to the sizes specified in the project directions. Here's what to do next:

1. Press one long edge of each pillow back ½" to the wrong side. Tuck in the raw edge to meet the fold and press again. Topstitch.

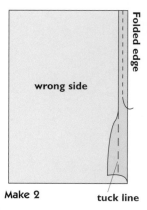

2. Place the two pillow backs right side up, overlapping the finished edges so that the overall measurement is the same as the pillow front. Baste the outside edges together where they overlap.

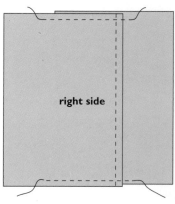

3. Place the pillow front and back right sides together. Machine-stitch ¼" from the edge all around. Trim the corners diagonally, and turn right side out. Insert the pillow form through the back opening.

Forest Friends Baby Quilt

Designed by Jean Wells and Lawry Thorn; 44" x 53½"

Soft flannels in pastel shades remind us of spring's first pussy willows. Baby forest animals occupy the larger squares in this embroidered and pieced quilt. To simplify the quiltmaking process, try using fusible appliqués or patterned fabrics in place of the embroidered blocks, or substitute plain fabric strips for the Flying Geese.

Materials

Flannel fabrics:

⅝ yard pale yellow check for embroidery background

¾ yard medium green for embroidery and Flying Geese backgrounds

⅛ yard each two different light greens for Double Four-Patch blocks

⅛ yard each three different lavenders for Double Four-Patch blocks

⅜ yard pale yellow print for Flying Geese

½ yard purple for sashing

¾ yard dark green for border

2¾ yards backing

½ yard for binding

48" x 58" batting

Embroidery floss:

dark gray (DMC #535)

medium gray (DMC #647)

dark brown (DMC #3031)

light brown (DMC #434)

reddish brown (DMC #975)

pine green (DMC #895)

dark sage (DMC #3362)

medium sage (DMC #3363)

light sage (DMC #3364)

BASIC INSTRUCTIONS

Embroidery Design Transfer (page 12)

Backstitch (page 13)

Four-Patch (page 14)

Double Four-Patch (page 15)

Double Half-Square Triangles (page 18)

Flying Geese (page 18)

Finishing a Quilt (page 23)

Cutting

From the pale yellow check, cut two 9½" x 42" strips; cut into five 9½" squares for the embroidery background.

From the medium green, cut two 5" x 42" strips; cut into six 5" x 11¾" rectangles for the embroidery background. Also cut five 2¾" x 42" strips; cut into sixty 2¾" squares for the Flying Geese units.

From each light green, cut one 5" x 42" strip; cut six 5" squares from one light green strip and four 5" squares from the other light green strip for the Double Four-Patch blocks.

From each lavender, cut one 2¾" x 42" strip for the Four-Patch units.

From the pale yellow print, cut four 2¾" x 42" strips; cut into thirty 2¾" x 5" rectangles for the Flying Geese units. For variety, cut some of the rectangles from the leftover pale yellow check instead.

From the purple, cut nine 1½" x 42" strips and sew together into one long strip; cut into six 1½" x 45½" strips for the vertical sashing and two 1½" x 38" strips for the top and bottom sashing.

From the dark green, cut five 3½" x 42" strips and sew together into one long strip; cut two 3½" x 47½" strips for the side borders and two 3½" x 44" strips for the top and bottom borders.

Assembly

1. Transfer the bunny, bear, squirrel, deer, and chickadee patterns (pages 29–32 and 109) to the five 9½" pale yellow check squares. Transfer the pine bough pattern (page 33) to the six 5" x 11¾" medium green rectangles. Embroider the marked lines of each design in backstitch, using the floss colors indicated on the patterns. Set aside.

2. Cut each 2¾" x 42" lavender strip in half. Stitch the six strips together in pairs, to make three different fabric combinations. Cut each double-strip into seven 2¾" segments, for 21 segments total (you will use 20).

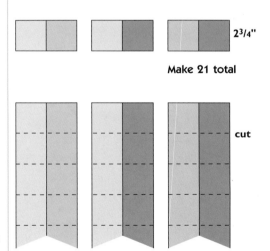

2¾"

Make 21 total

cut

3. Group the segments together in pairs so that adjacent fabrics do not match (see the quilt photograph on page 26). Stitch together to make 10 Four-Patch units.

Make 10 assorted

4. Join the Four-Patch units with the 5" light green squares to make 5 Double Four-Patch blocks. Set aside.

9" (finished)

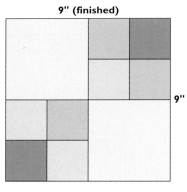

9"

Make 5

5. Stitch two 2¾" medium green squares to each 2¾" x 5" pale yellow print or check rectangle to make 30 double half-square triangles. Join the double half-square triangles together to make 7 Flying Geese units: 1 two-piece unit, 2 three-piece units, 3 five-piece units, and 1 seven-piece unit.

Make 30

Join to make Flying Geese units

6. Lay out all the pieces, referring to the quilt photograph (page 26) and quilt diagram. Arrange the embroidered pine bough rectangles and the Flying Geese units in three columns and the embroidered animal and chickadee blocks and the Double Four-Patch blocks in two columns. Stitch the pieces in each column together. Press.

7. Stitch vertical sashing strips to the sides of each Flying Geese column. Press toward the sashing. Join the remaining columns in between. Press.

Add the top and bottom sashing. Press. Add the side borders. Press. Add the top and bottom borders. Press.

8. Layer and finish the quilt. *Forest Friends* features diagonal machine quilting, which forms an "X" pattern in the plain blocks, and in-the-ditch quilting to define the sashing strips and block outlines. A continuous stitching line curves alongside the Flying Geese triangles. The embroidered designs are outline-quilted.

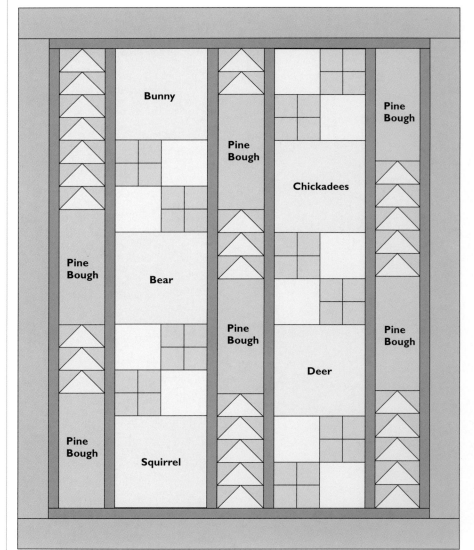

Quilt Diagram

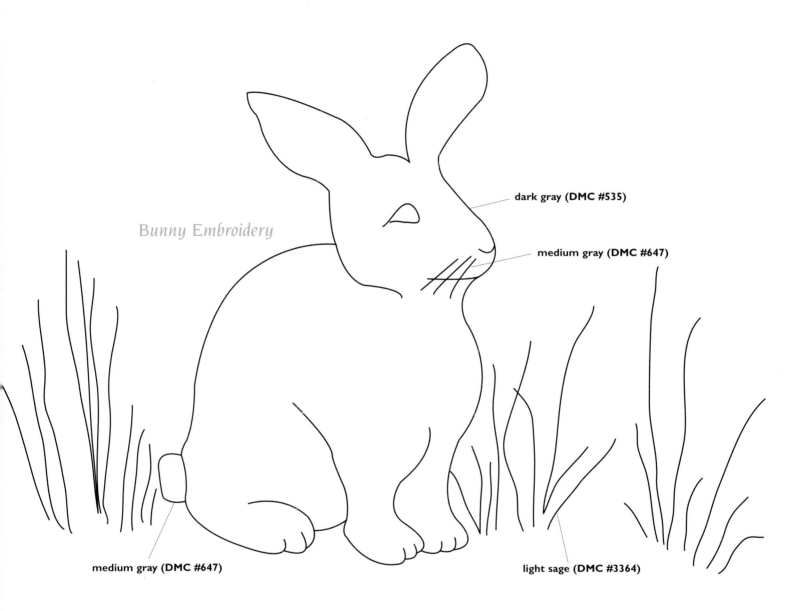

Bunny Embroidery

dark gray (DMC #535)

medium gray (DMC #647)

medium gray (DMC #647)

light sage (DMC #3364)

Forest Friends Baby Quilt

Photocopy at 70% for the Carryall (page 38)

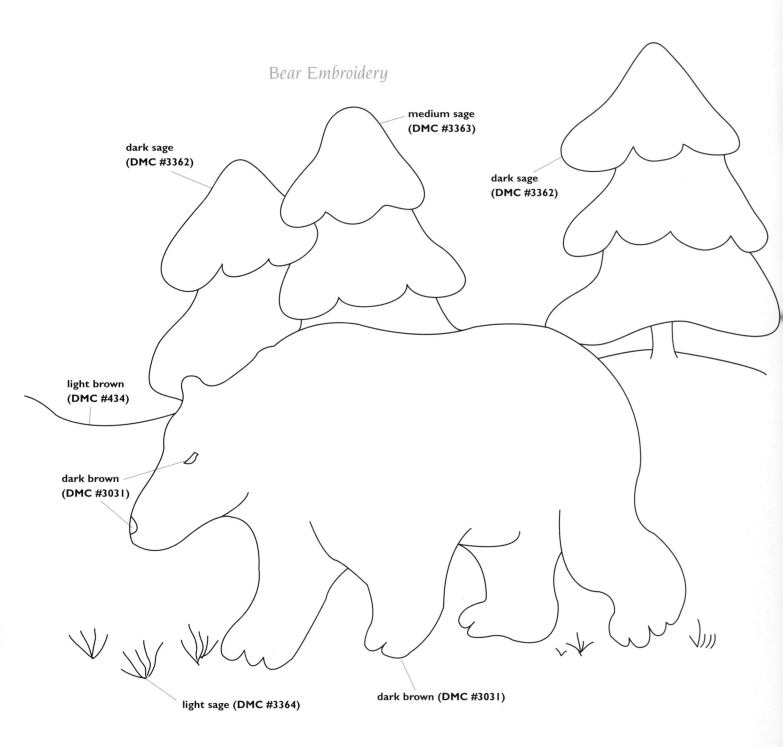

Bear Embroidery

medium sage
(DMC #3363)

dark sage
(DMC #3362)

dark sage
(DMC #3362)

light brown
(DMC #434)

dark brown
(DMC #3031)

light sage (DMC #3364)

dark brown (DMC #3031)

Forest Friends Baby Quilt

Use this pattern as an appliqué design for the *Lakeside* quilt Animal Tracks blocks (page 49).

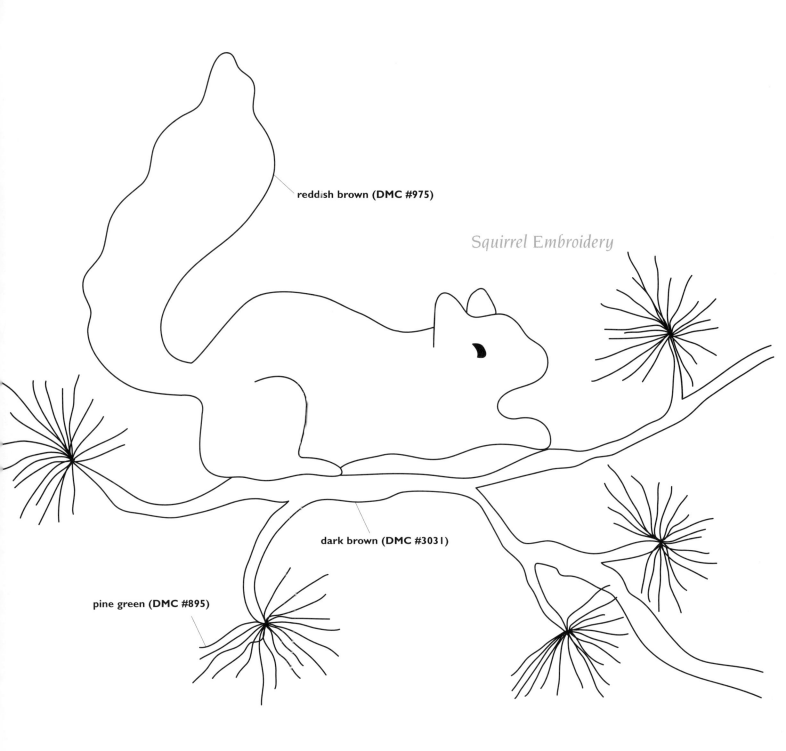

reddish brown (DMC #975)

Squirrel Embroidery

dark brown (DMC #3031)

pine green (DMC #895)

Forest Friends Baby Quilt

Use this pattern as an appliqué design for the *Lakeside* quilt Animal Tracks blocks (page 49).

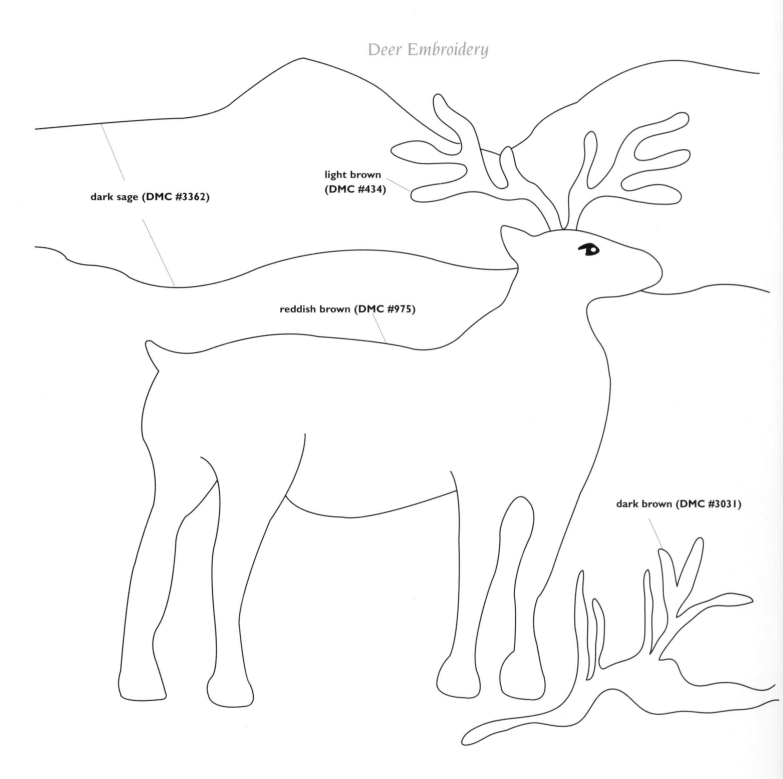

Deer Embroidery

dark sage (DMC #3362)

light brown
(DMC #434)

reddish brown (DMC #975)

dark brown (DMC #3031)

Forest Friends Baby Quilt

Use this pattern as an appliqué design for the *Lakeside* quilt Animal Tracks blocks (page 49).

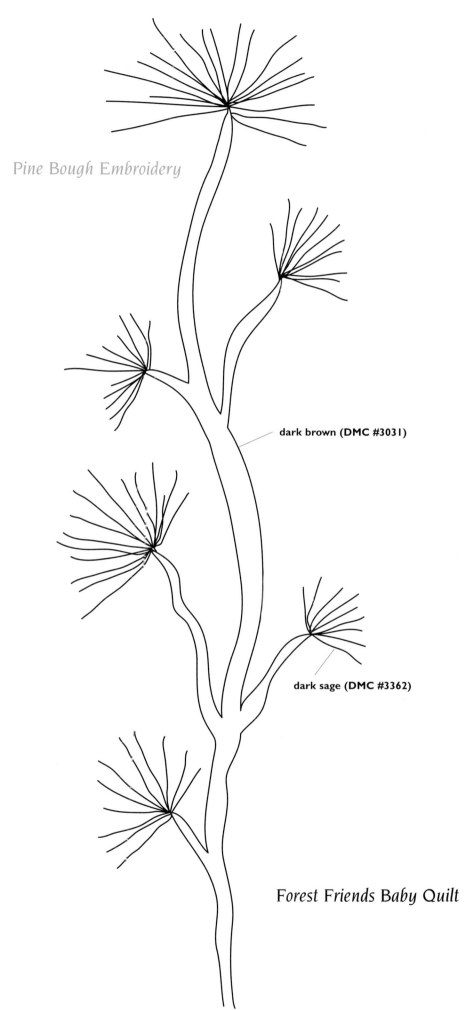

Pine Bough Embroidery

dark brown (DMC #3031)

dark sage (DMC #3362)

Forest Friends Baby Quilt

Designed by Jean Wells and Lawry Thorn; 88$\frac{1}{2}$" x 88$\frac{1}{2}$"

One sign of early spring is the soft, fresh greens of flowers pushing their way through a lingering blanket of snow. We tried to capture this moment in *Pine Star*, by combining greens with creamy whites. The large patchwork shapes will speed you through the piecing.

Materials

Flannel fabrics:

1 yard medium green print for Pine Star and Pathways blocks

$3/8$ yard dark green print for Pine Star block

$5/8$ yard light tan print for Pine Star block

$2^1/2$ yards pine green print for Pine Star block and outside border

$1^5/8$ yards medium tan print for Pathways and Pine Tree blocks

1 yard tree green print for Pine Tree blocks

$2^5/8$ yards golden tan print for borders

$7^3/4$ yards backing

$1/2$ yard for binding

93" x 93" batting

Cutting

PINE STAR BLOCK

Prepare templates A and D (page 37), enlarging 200%.

From the medium green print, cut 4 squares using template A.

From the dark green print, cut one $9^1/4$" square; cut diagonally in both directions for 4 quarter-square triangles (B).

From the light tan print, cut one $17^1/4$" square; cut diagonally in both directions for 4 quarter-square triangles (C). Also cut four $8^1/2$" squares (E).

From the pine green print, cut 4 pieces using template D.

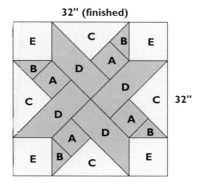

32" (finished)

32"

Pine Star Block Diagram

PATHWAYS BLOCKS

From the medium green print, cut two $8^1/2$" x 42" strips; cut into eight $8^1/2$" squares (A). Cut two $4^1/2$" x 42" strips; cut into sixteen $4^1/2$" squares (C).

From the medium tan print, cut two $3^1/2$" x 42" strips; cut into sixteen $4^1/2$" x $8^1/2$" rectangles (B). Cut two $12^1/2$" x 42" strips; cut into sixteen $4^1/2$" x $12^1/2$" rectangles (D).

16" (finished)

16"

Pathways Block Diagram

PINE TREE BLOCKS

Prepare templates A through H (pages 88–89), enlarging 200%. Trim the seam allowance on the enlarged templates to $1/4$".

From the tree green print, cut 4 each of A, B, C, D, and E.

From the medium tan print, cut 8 each (reverse 4) of F, G, and H.

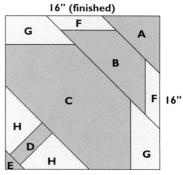

16" (finished)

16"

Pine Tree Block Diagram

INNER BORDER

From the golden tan print, cut seven $4^1/2$" x 42" strips and sew together into one long strip; cut two $4^1/2$" x $64^1/2$" strips for the side inner borders and two $4^1/2$" x $72^1/2$" strips for the top and bottom inner borders.

FLYING GEESE BORDER

From the pine green print, cut seven $8^1/2$" x 42" strips; cut into twenty $4^1/2$" x $8^1/2$" rectangles (A), four $8^1/2$" x $16^1/2$" rectangles (B), and four $8^1/2$" x $20^1/2$" rectangles (C). Cut three $4^1/2$" x 42" strips; cut into twenty-four $4^1/2$" squares.

From the golden tan print, cut three $8^1/2$" x 42" strips; cut into seven $4^1/2$" x $8^1/2$" rectangles (D), five $8^1/2$" squares (E), one $8^1/2$" x $12^1/2$" rectangle (F), and one $8^1/2$" x $16^1/2$" rectangle (G). Cut seven $4^1/2$" x 42" strips; cut into fifty-six $4^1/2$" squares.

Assembly

1. Make 1 Pine Star block.

2. Make 4 Pine Tree blocks.

3. Make 8 Pathways blocks, arranging 4 blocks with the C squares at the top right and lower left corners and 4 blocks with the C squares at the top left and lower right corners. Stitch the blocks together in mirror-image pairs.

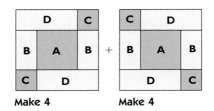

Make 4   **Make 4**

4. Join 2 Pathways units to the top and bottom edges of the Pine Star block.

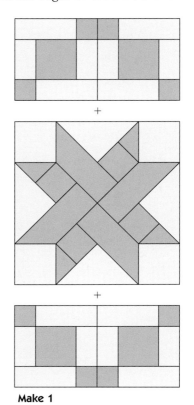

Make 1

5. Join 2 Pine Tree blocks to each remaining Pathways unit.

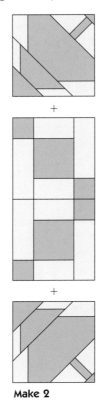

Make 2

6. Join the Pine Star and Pine Tree units together, as shown in the quilt photograph (page 34) and quilt diagram (page 37). Add the side inner borders. Press. Add the top and bottom inner borders. Press.

7. Stitch two 4½" golden tan print squares to each pine green print A rectangle to make 20 A double half-square triangles. Reverse the colors to make 5 D double half-square triangles. Set aside the remaining two D rectangles.

Make 20   **Make 5**

8. Use the double half-square triangle technique to stitch two 4½" pine green squares to one end of each

golden tan E, F, and G rectangle. The resulting units will resemble "arrows" in three different lengths.

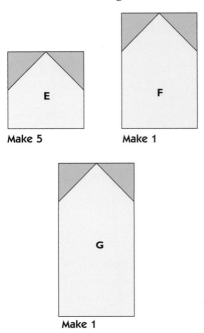

Make 5   **Make 1**

Make 1

9. Repeat step 8, reversing the colors, to make arrows with the remaining Flying Geese pieces.

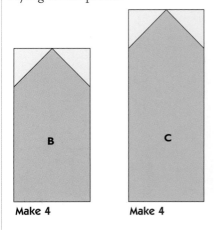

Make 4   **Make 4**

10. Arrange the double half-square triangles, arrows, and remaining D rectangles into the side, top, and bottom Flying Geese borders, as shown in the quilt diagram (page 37). Stitch the pieces for each border together. Add the side borders to the quilt. Press. Add the top and bottom borders. Press.

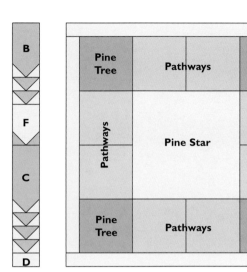

Quilt Diagram

11. Layer and finish the quilt. P*ine Star* features diagonal machine quilting, which forms a diamond pattern in the Pathways blocks. In-the-ditch and outline quilting define the basic patchwork shapes and block outlines. The extra-large patchwork shapes are filled in with a free-form leaf and swirl design that carries out the woodsy theme.

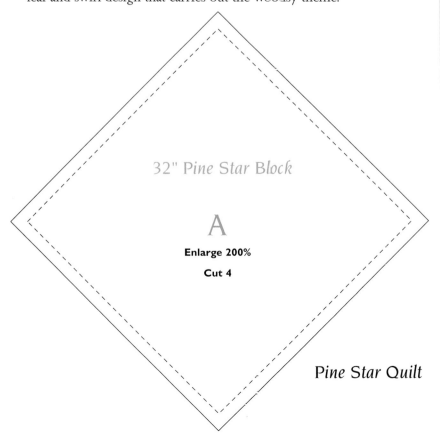

32" *Pine Star Block*

A

Enlarge 200%

Cut 4

Pine Star Quilt

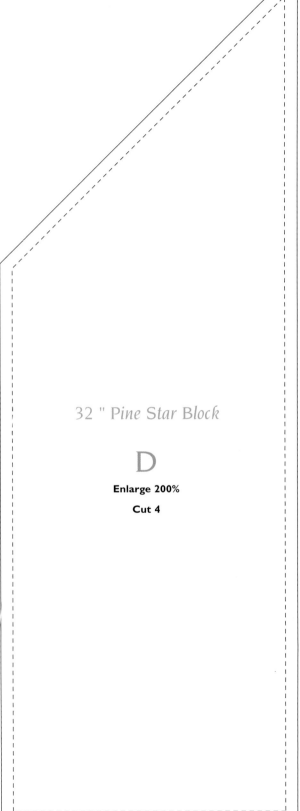

32 " *Pine Star Block*

D

Enlarge 200%

Cut 4

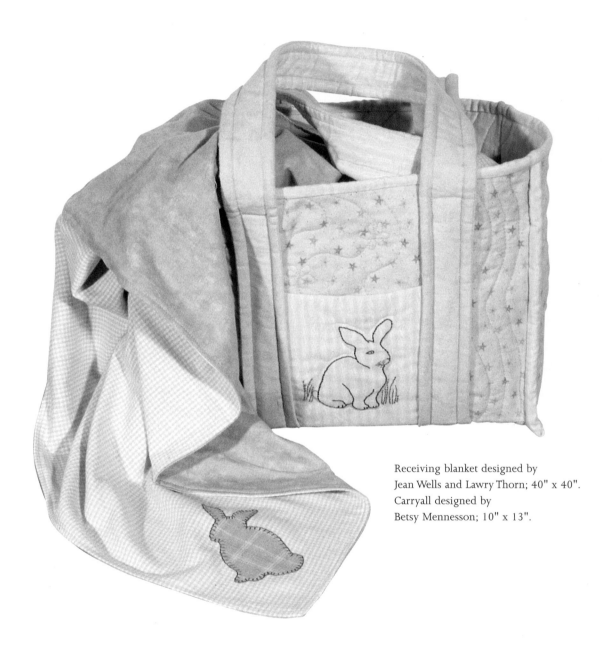

Receiving blanket designed by
Jean Wells and Lawry Thorn; 40" x 40".
Carryall designed by
Betsy Mennesson; 10" x 13".

Cutting

From the pale yellow check and the lavender print, cut one 41" square each.

Photocopy the bunny pattern on page 77 at 125%, and prepare a lavender plaid fusible appliqué.

Assembly

1. Lay the pale yellow check flannel square right side up. Position the lavender bunny appliqué in one corner, right side up and about $1^3/4$" in from the edges. Fuse in place. Work buttonhole stitch in lavender floss around the edge of the appliqué.

2. Place both flannel squares right sides together. Starting at the middle of one edge, stitch $1/2$" from the edge all around, pivoting at the corners. Stop about 5" from the starting point, leaving an opening for turning. Trim the corners diagonally. Turn right side out.

3. Press the edges all around. Fold in the seam allowances at the opening, press, and slip-stitch closed. Topstitch $1/4$" from the edge all around.

QUILTER'S TIP

As an alternative to topstitching, try one of your machine's pretty embroidery stitches. Test the stitch on scrap fabric first.

Years ago, when our children were born, we made our own receiving blankets from flannel. As our daughters grew older, they used the blankets for their dolls. We still have those blankets to this day. A receiving blanket with your hand-embroidered appliqué makes a welcome gift for a new baby and is sure to inspire sentimental memories for the next generation.

Materials

Flannel fabrics:

$1^1/4$ yards pale yellow check for front

$1^1/4$ yards lavender print for back

4" x 5" lavender plaid for appliqué

Paper-backed fusible web

Lavender embroidery floss (DMC #3746)

BASIC INSTRUCTIONS

Buttonhole Stitch Appliqué (page 10)

This roomy, rectangular tote is fully lined and has pockets inside and out. It is perfect for carrying baby's important things. Embroider a bunny on the outside pocket, or substitute one of the other designs found throughout the book.

Materials

Flannel fabrics:

$1/2$ yard pale green print for main and side panels

$1/4$ yard pale green solid for handles

$1^1/4$ yards pale yellow stripe for lining, pockets, and binding

$3/4$ yard lightweight batting

Embroidery floss:

dark gray (DMC #535)

medium gray (DMC #647)

light sage (DMC #3364)

BASIC INSTRUCTIONS

Embroidery Design Transfer (page 12)

Backstitch (page 13)

French Knot (page 13)

Cutting

From the pale green print, cut one 13½" x 26½" rectangle for the main panel and two 6½" x 10½" rectangles for the side panels.

From the pale green solid, cut three 2½" x 42" strips for the handles.

From the pale yellow stripe, cut one lining piece to match each pale green piece (3 rectangles and 3 strips), one 5½" x 13" outside pocket, two 6½" x 15" small inside pockets, and three 2" x 42" strips for the binding.

From the batting, cut one piece to match each pale green piece (3 rectangles and 3 strips) and one 5½" x 6½" rectangle for the outside pocket.

Assembly

1. Photocopy the *Forest Friends* bunny pattern (page 29) at 70% of the original size. Fold the outside pale yellow pocket in half crosswise, right side out. Press to set the fold, which will become the top edge of the pocket. Open out the pocket, lay it right side up, and transfer the bunny and a bit of the grass to the pocket front.

2. Embroider the pocket design in backstitch, using dark gray floss for the bunny body and eye (the pupil is a French knot), medium gray floss for the whiskers and tail, and light sage floss for the grass.

3. Refold the embroidered pocket right side out. Sandwich the 5½" x 6½" batting in between the layers, and baste the raw edges together. Outline-quilt the bunny by machine.

4. Layer the pale green print main panel and its pale yellow stripe lining wrong sides together, sandwiching the batting in between. Pin. Repeat to layer the two side panels. Machine-quilt the layers together, using a freestyle design that coordinates with the fabric print. In our project, Betsy quilted wavy lines, small flowers, and small stars.

5. Lay the main panel flat, right side up. Measure and mark two parallel lines, 10¼" from each short edge and 6" apart, to define the base of the carryall. Machine-stitch on both lines through all layers. Position the bunny pocket upside down and facedown on the main panel as shown, so that the lower edge overlaps one of the stitching lines by ½". Machine-stitch the pocket to the main panel, over the previous stitching. Fold up the pocket and baste the side edges.

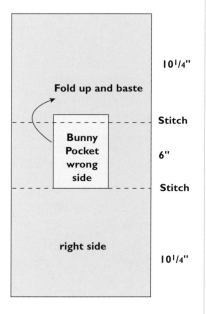

6. Stitch the pale green strips together to make one long strip; trim to 2½" x 93½". Repeat with the pale yellow strips. Butt and whipstitch the batting strips together, and trim to the same length.

7. Place the two long flannel strips right sides together. Slip the batting underneath. Stitch down one long edge through all layers, using a ¼" seam allowance. Stitch the opposite edge, starting and stopping 5" from each end. Trim the batting close to the stitching lines. Turn the strip right side out, using a safety pin as a bodkin. The fuzzy surface on the flannel will make turning difficult, so be patient.

8. Place the ends of the strip right sides together and stitch to form a continuous loop. Trim the batting close to the stitching line. Press the seam open. Refold the strip, tuck in the raw edges, and press. Slip-stitch the open edge closed. Topstitch ½" from both edges all around.

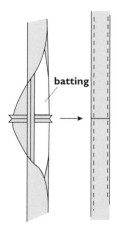

9. Use pins to mark the handle loop into four segments: 21", 26½", 21", 26½". Position the handle on the main panel, pale green side up, so the two longer segments are 2½" in from the outside edges and the two shorter segments form the handles. Pin in place, concealing the raw edges of the outside pocket. Topstitch over the previous topstitching, securing the pocket as you go. When you are 1" from the top edge of the panel, stop with your needle in the down position. Pivot, stitch straight across the handle, pivot again, and resume stitching down the opposite side. Continue until both handle loops are stitched down.

10. Lay each side panel lining side up. Fold each inside pocket in half crosswise, right side out, and press. Position a pocket on each side panel, aligning the side and bottom edges. Baste in place. Pin the side panels to the main panel, lining sides together. Machine-stitch with a ¼" seam allowance, pivoting at the corners.

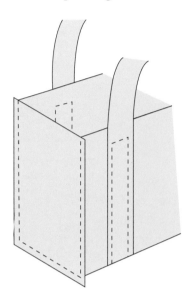

11. Join the binding strips together to make one long strip. Press both long edges ¼" to the wrong side. To bind the exposed seam allowances, place the binding on the main panel, right sides together and raw edges matching, and stitch through all layers, making a small tuck at each corner. Trim off the excess binding strip even with the top edge. Fold the binding over the seam allowance, line up the pressed fold on the stitching line, and slip-stitch in place. Bind the top raw edge of the carryall last.

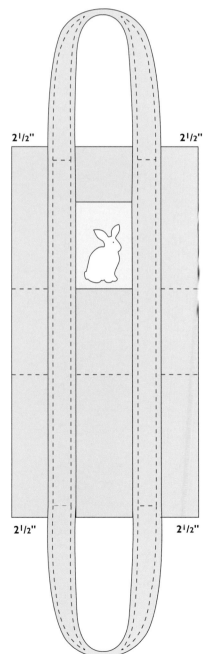

2½"   2½"

2½"   2½"

Designed by Jean Wells and Lawry Thorn; 24" x 24"

This ample floor cushion combines four buttonhole stitch animal appliqués and two easy-to-piece block designs. It makes a handy accessory in the nursery.

Materials

Flannel fabrics:
   ½ yard yellow plaid for appliquéd and pieced blocks
   ¼ yard green for pieced blocks
   ¼ yard lilac for appliqués
   ¾ yard solid for pillow back
Paper-backed fusible web

24" pillow form
Lilac embroidery floss (DMC #208)

BASIC INSTRUCTIONS

Buttonhole Stitch Appliqué (page 10)
French Knot (page 13)
Pathways (page 17)
Finishing a Pillow (page 24)

Cutting

From the yellow plaid, cut one 8½" x 42" strip; cut into four 8½" squares for the appliquéd blocks. Cut one 2½" x 42" strip (B) and one 6½" x 42" strip (D) for the Pathways blocks.

From the green, cut one 4½" x 42" strip (A) and one 2½" x 42" strip (C) for the Pathways blocks. The pieces for the center block will be cut later from these same strips.

Use the patterns on pages 44–45 to prepare the fusible appliqués: 1 bunny, 1 squirrel, 1 deer, and 1 bear, all in lilac.

From the pillow back fabric, cut two 24½" x 16" rectangles.

Assembly

1. Center each animal appliqué on an 8½" yellow plaid square and fuse in place. Work buttonhole stitch in lilac floss around each appliqué. Make French knot eyes.

2. Cut the yellow plaid B strip in half and stitch to the sides of the green A strip. Press toward the darker fabric. Cut into five 4½" segments.

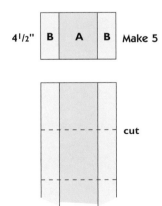

3. Cut one 10" piece each from strips C and D and set aside. Stitch the remainder of the C and D strips together. Press. Cut into eight 2½" segments.

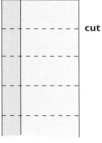

4. Make 4 Pathways blocks (2 in mirror image) by joining the CD units to four of the BAB units. Press toward the block's outer edge.

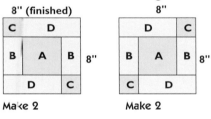

Pathways Blocks

5. From the reserved green and yellow strips, cut four 2½" green squares (C) and two 2½" x 4½" yellow rectangles (B). Stitch 2 C squares to each B. Join the CBC units to the remaining BAB unit to complete the center block. Press toward the block's outer edge.

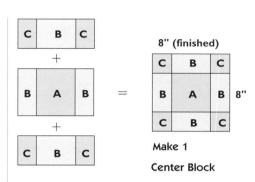

Make 1
Center Block

6. Arrange the nine blocks as shown in the pillow photograph (page 42) and pillow diagram. Use the Nine-Patch construction (page 15) to stitch the blocks together in rows, and then join the rows. Remember to press after each addition.

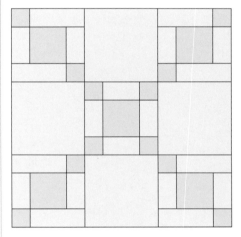

Pillow Diagram

7. Complete the pillow following the directions on page 24.

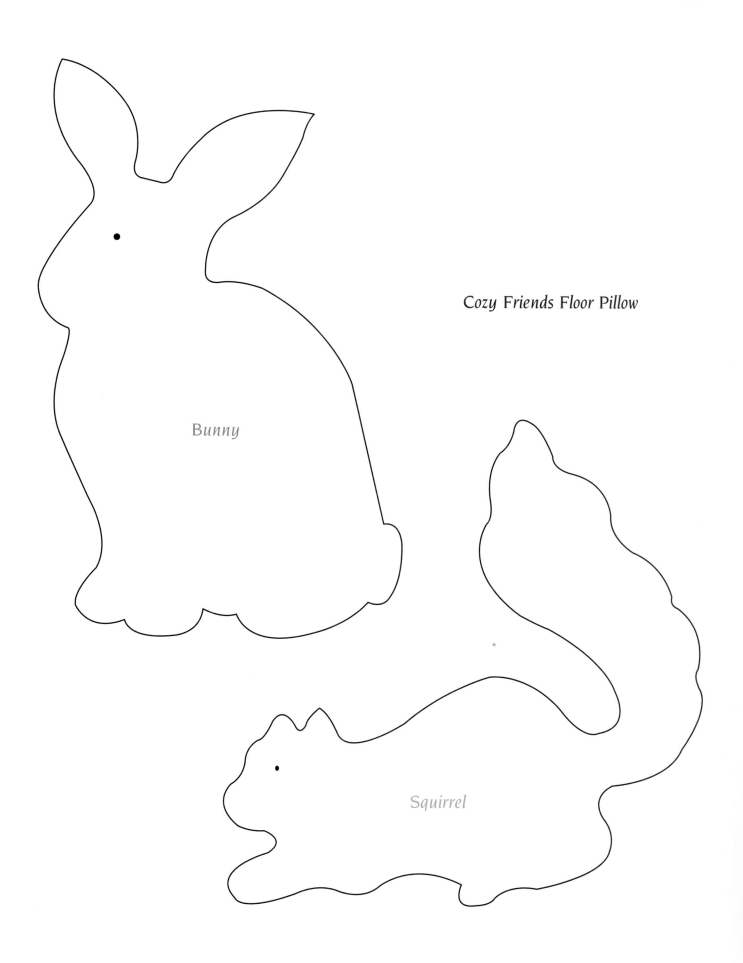

Cozy Friends Floor Pillow

Bunny

Squirrel

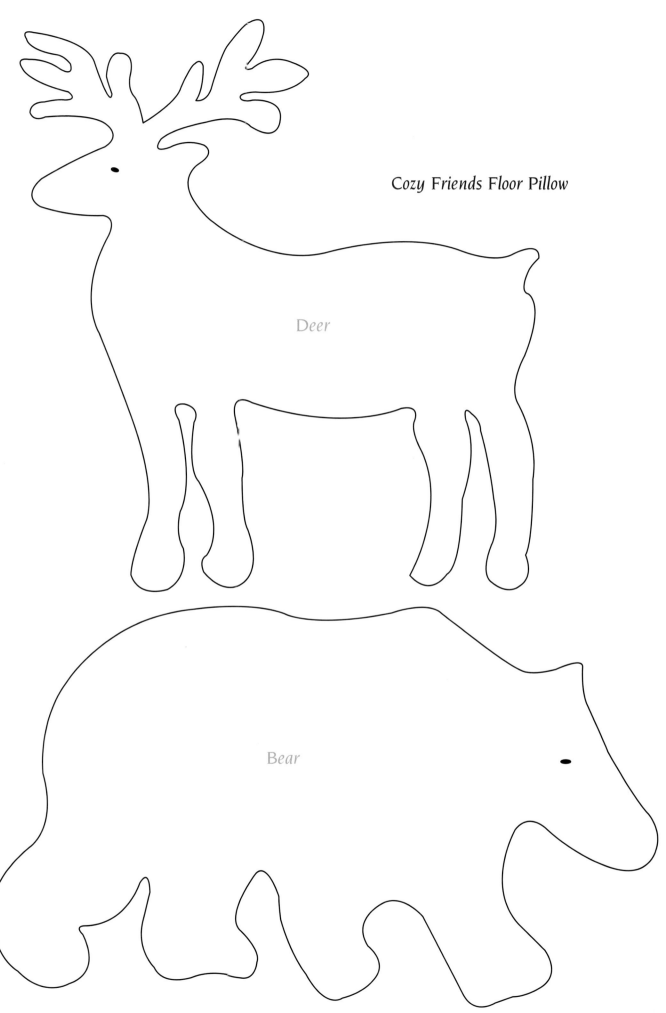

Cozy Friends Floor Pillow

Deer

Bear

SUMMER

Lakeside Quilt

Designed by Jean Wells and Lawry Thorn; 77" x 103"

Vibrant, clear colors bring lively pieced, embroidered, and buttonhole stitch blocks into sharp focus on our outdoorsy signature quilt. Just looking at the designs transports us to summertime in Sisters—a season for walking through pine forests, listening to mountain streams gurgling over the rocks, and breathing in the clean, pine-scented air. On cool summer evenings, we can wrap *Lakeside* around our shoulders, sit out on the porch, and gaze up at stars that seem close enough to touch.

Materials

Flannel fabrics:

$1^3/_4$ yards light tan print for backgrounds, Animal Tracks blocks, and Pathways blocks

Assorted print and plaid scraps for appliqués and piecing (we used browns, blues, greens, golds, reds, and black)

$1^5/_8$ yards blue sky print for background

$1^3/_4$ yards blue print for mountains, checkerboard strips, and middle border

$1/_4$ yard each of four different green prints and plaids for mountain and tree appliqués, pinecones border, fish border, and Pine Bough Logs

$1/_2$ yard dark blue check for mountains and Pine Star

$1^1/_2$ yards light tan check for snowcaps, background, Pine Bough Logs, and Flying Geese

$1^3/_8$ yards red check for fish border, Pine Stars, and outer border

$5/_8$ yard black for fish border and inner border

$1/_4$ yard dark blue print for Animal Tracks "night bear" background

$1/_2$ yard red for Animal Tracks and Pine Bough Logs

$1/_4$ yard dark red check for Pathways

$7/_8$ yard gold print for Pine Stars, checkerboard strips, and embroidery background

$3/_8$ yard light blue for background

$1/_4$ yard red print for Pine Stars

$1/_4$ yard dark gold print for Pine Trees background

$1/_2$ yard dark rust for Flying Geese

$6^1/_4$ yards backing

$1/_2$ yard for binding

Paper-backed fusible web

81" x 107" batting

Embroidery floss:

reddish brown (DMC #975)

dark brown (DMC #3031)

pine green (DMC #895)

black (DMC #310)

Cutting

CABIN BLOCK

From the light tan print, cut one $16^1/_2$" square for the background.

Use the patterns on pages 57 and 70–71 and the flannel scraps to prepare the fusible appliqués: 1 cabin, 1 door, 1 window, 1 gable, 1 roof, 5 fir trees, 1 deer, 1 bear, and 3 stepping stones. See the quilt photograph (page 47) for color ideas.

MOUNTAINS UNIT

From the blue sky print, cut two $8^1/_2$" x 42" strips and sew together into one long strip; cut into one $8^1/_2$" x $48^1/_2$" rectangle for the background.

Photocopy the patterns on pages 56–57 at 200%, and prepare the fusible appliqués: 4 blue print A mountains, 2 green print B mountains, 1 green plaid C mountain, 1 green print C mountain, 2 blue print D mountains, 1 dark blue check D mountain, 4 light tan check A snowcaps, and 3 light tan check D snowcaps.

PINECONES BLOCK

From the light tan check, cut one $8^1/_2$" square for the background.

From a green print, cut one $2^1/_2$" x 42" strip; cut into two $2^1/_2$" x $8^1/_2$" strips and two $2^1/_2$" x $12^1/_2$" strips for the border.

Use the embroidery pattern on page 116 and follow the tip on page 50 to prepare the fusible appliqués: Make 2 brown print pinecones and 1 dark brown branch, adapting the pattern as desired.

FISH UNITS (2)

From the light tan print, cut one $4\frac{1}{2}$" x $12\frac{1}{2}$" rectangle for the single-fish background.

From the blue sky print, cut one $8\frac{1}{2}$" x $32\frac{1}{2}$" rectangle for the five-fish background.

From the red check and the black, cut two $2\frac{1}{2}$" x 42" strips each; cut each strip into one $2\frac{1}{2}$" x 8" strip and one $2\frac{1}{2}$" x $32\frac{1}{2}$" strip for the five-fish border.

From a green print, cut four $4\frac{1}{2}$" squares for the five-fish border.

Use the large fish pattern on page 58 to prepare 6 fusible appliqués in assorted colors (we chose red plaid, gold, and green).

ANIMAL TRACKS BLOCKS (5)

From the blue sky print, cut one $8\frac{1}{2}$" x 42" strip; cut into four $8\frac{1}{2}$" squares for the appliqué background (the block centers).

From the dark blue print, cut one $8\frac{1}{2}$" square for the "night bear" appliqué background (the block center).

Use the embroidery patterns on pages 30–32 and follow the tip on page 50 to prepare the fusible appliqués. Make 1 deer, 1 deer landscape, 1 squirrel, 1 branch, 2 bears (reverse 1), 2 bear landscapes (reverse 1), and 6 pine trees (make a separate appliqué for each tree tier). In addition, use the patterns on pages 58 and 77 to prepare 1 medium and 2 small fish appliqués. See the quilt photograph (page 47) for color ideas.

From the light tan print, cut two $2\frac{1}{2}$" x 42" strips; cut into twenty $2\frac{1}{2}$" squares for the block corners.

Place the remaining light tan print and red flannel right sides together, selvages matching. Cut three $2\frac{7}{8}$" x 42" strips through both layers; cut into forty $2\frac{7}{8}$" squares; cut in half diagonally for 80 half-square triangle pairs for the block borders. Do not separate the pairs; they are ready for sewing.

PINE BOUGH LOGS BLOCKS (4)

From the light tan check, cut one $2\frac{1}{2}$" x 42" strip (A) and two $4\frac{1}{2}$" x 42" strips (D).

From a green print, cut one $2\frac{1}{2}$" x 42" strip (B1) and one $4\frac{1}{2}$" x 42" strip (B2).

From the red, cut one $1\frac{1}{2}$" x 42" strip (C) and one $2\frac{1}{2}$" x 42" strip (E).

PATHWAYS BLOCKS (4)

From the light tan print, cut one 3" x 42" strip (A), one 2" x 42" strip (B), and one $7\frac{1}{2}$" x 42" strip (D); cut strip B into eight 2" x $5\frac{1}{2}$" rectangles.

From the dark red check, cut one 3" x 42" strip (A) and one 2" x 42" strip (C).

PINE STAR BLOCKS (6)

Prepare templates A and D (page 54), photocopying at 100%.

From the dark blue check, cut 24 squares using template A.

From the gold print, cut one $3\frac{1}{4}$ x 42" strip; cut into six $3\frac{1}{4}$" squares; cut each square diagonally in both directions for 24 quarter-square triangles (B).

From the light blue, cut one $5\frac{1}{4}$" x 42" strip; cut into six $5\frac{1}{4}$" squares; cut each square diagonally in both directions for 24 quarter-square triangles (C). Also cut two $2\frac{1}{2}$" x 42" strips; cut into twenty-four $2\frac{1}{2}$" squares (E).

From the red check and the red print, cut 12 pieces each using template D (24 total).

PINE TREE BLOCKS (5) AND SETTING TRIANGLES

Prepare templates A through H (pages 88–89), photocopying at 100%.

From the various green prints and plaids, cut 5 matching sets of A, B, and C.

From a brown print, cut 5 D and 5 E.

From the dark gold print, cut 10 each (reverse 5) of F, G, and H.

From the blue sky print, cut two $13\frac{1}{2}$" squares; cut diagonally in both directions for 8 quarter-square triangles (discard 2). Also cut four $8\frac{1}{4}$" squares; cut in half diagonally for 8 half-square triangles to use in the corners.

CHECKERBOARD STRIPS

From the blue print and the gold print, cut six $2\frac{1}{2}$" x 42" strips each.

FLYING GEESE UNITS

From the dark rust, cut three $4\frac{1}{2}$" x 42" strips; cut into thirty-seven $2\frac{1}{2}$" x $4\frac{1}{2}$" rectangles.

From the light tan check, cut five $2\frac{1}{2}$" x 42" strips; cut into seventy-four $2\frac{1}{2}$" squares. Also cut four $4\frac{1}{2}$" x 42" strips; cut into 12 rectangles for fillers: one $4\frac{1}{2}$" x $10\frac{1}{2}$" (A), one 4½" x 8½" (B), one 4½" x 7½" (C), three 4½" x 6½" (D), one 4½" x 5½" (E), two 4½" x 4½" (F), and three 4½" x 2½" (G).

EMBROIDERED UNITS

From the light tan print, cut one 4½" x 10½" strip (H), one 4½" x 26½" strip (I), one 6½" x 18½" strip (K), and one 4½" x 40½" strip (L). From the gold print, cut two 4½" x 20½" strips (J).

BORDERS

From the black, cut eight 1½" x 42" strips and sew together into one long strip; cut two 1½" x 88½" strips for the side inner borders and two 1½" x 68½" strips for the top and bottom inner borders.

From the blue print, cut eight 2¼" x 42" strips and sew together into one long strip; cut two 2¼" x 90½" strips for the side middle borders and two 2½" x 72½" strips for the top and bottom middle borders.

From the red check, cut nine 4" x 42" strips and sew together into one long strip; cut two 4" x 94½" strips for the side outer borders and two 4" x 76½" strips for the top and bottom outer borders.

QUILTER'S TIP

To reverse an embroidery pattern for fusible appliqué, trace the image outline only and then turn the tracing over and go over the design line from the wrong side.

Assembly

APPLIQUÉD BLOCKS AND UNITS

1. Arrange the appliqués for the cabin block, mountains unit, pinecones block, five-fish unit, single-fish unit, and five Animal Tracks blocks on the appropriate background fabrics. Overlap the pieces as shown in the color photograph (page 47) and in the individual patterns to create the various scenes. When you are satisfied with the placement, fuse the appliqués in place, working from background to foreground.

2. Work buttonhole stitch in black floss around all of the appliqués, either now or—if you prefer—when the quilt is further assembled.

3. To complete the pinecones block, stitch a 2½" x 8½" green print strip to each side edge. Press. Stitch the 2½" x 12½" green print strips to the top and bottom edges. Press. Embroider green pine needles on the branch in stem stitch as desired.

4. To complete the five-fish unit, stitch the red check and black border strips together in pairs. Press. Stitch a 4½" green square to both ends of each shorter border unit. Join the longer borders to the top and bottom edges of the appliquéd fish unit, with the red check strip on the inside. Press. Join the shorter units to the side edges, with the black strip on the inside. Press.

5. To complete the Animal Tracks blocks, stitch 80 half-square triangles together along the diagonal as paired. Press. Follow the basic instructions to assemble the blocks, using the five appliquéd squares from step 1 as the center units.

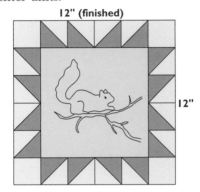

12" (finished)

12"

Animal Tracks with Appliquéd Center Unit
Make 5 assorted

PIECED BLOCKS AND UNITS

1. **Pine Bough Logs.** Cut strip B1 in half crosswise. Join to opposite edges of strip A, press, and cut into four 2½" segments. Cut strip C in half. Join to strip B2, press, and cut into eight 1½" segments. Cut strip E in half. Join to strip D, press, and cut into eight 2½" segments. From the remaining D strip, cut eight 2½" x 4½" pieces. Join all the pieces as described in the basic instructions to make 4 Pine Bough Logs blocks.

8" (finished)

E		D		E
	C	B	C	
D	B	A	B	D
	C	B	C	
E		D		E

8"

Pine Bough Logs
Make 4

2. **Pathways.** Stitch the light tan print and dark red check A strips together. Press. Cut into eight 3" segments. Join the segments together to make 4 Four-Patch units. Stitch the dark red check C and light tan print D strips together. Press. Cut into eight 2" segments. Treating the Four-Patch unit as A, join all the pieces as described in the basic instructions to make 4 Pathways blocks.

8" (finished)

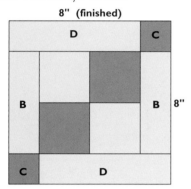

Pathways Variation
Make 4 (2 in mirror image)

3. **Pine Star.** Follow the basic instructions to make 6 blocks. Use 2 plaid and 2 solid D pieces in each block.

8" (finished)

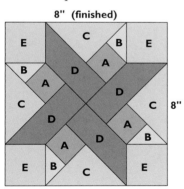

Pine Star
Make 6

4. **Pine Tree.** Follow the basic instructions to make 5 blocks.

8" (finished)

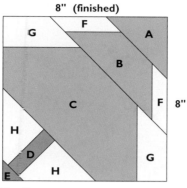

Pine Tree
Make 5

5. Stitch the Pine Bough Logs, Pathways, and Pine Star blocks together as shown to make 3 units.

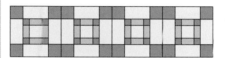

Pine Bough Logs Unit (4 blocks)

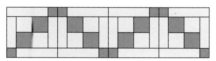

Pathways Unit (4 blocks)

Pine Star Unit (6 blocks)

6. Arrange the Pine Tree blocks on point in two groups—horizontal and vertical—and fill in the edges and corners with the blue setting triangles as shown. Stitch the setting triangles to the blocks, forming diagonal rows. Stitch the rows together, adding the corner triangles last. Trim the horizontal unit to 24½" x 12½". Trim the vertical unit to 12½" x 36½".

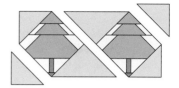

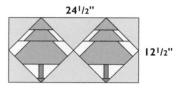

Pine Trees Horizontal Unit (2 blocks)

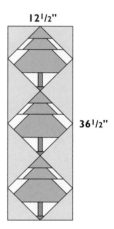

Pine Trees Vertical Unit (3 blocks)

7. **Checkerboard Strips.** Cut and set aside two 2½" squares each from a blue and a gold strip. Sew the blue and gold strips together in pairs. Press. Cut into ninety 2½" segments. Stitch the segments together, adding a single square as needed, to make the following checkerboard strips: two 1x4, two 1x6, one 1x7 (dark square at each end), two 1x8, one 1x9 (dark square at each end), one 1x11 (light square at each end), three 1x14, two 2x6, two 2x8, and one 2x12. Press after each addition.

1x8   2x4

Checkerboard Strips
Make 17 total

8. **Flying Geese.** Follow the basic instructions to make 37 double half-square triangle units. Join the triangle units and filler rectangles A through G as shown to make four Flying Geese units. Press.

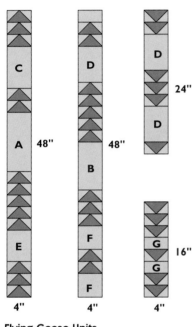

Flying Geese Units
Make 4

JOINING THE UNITS

1. Stitch a 2x4 checkerboard strip to the left edge of the mountains unit. Press. Stitch a 1x4 checkerboard strip to the right edge. Press. Stitch a 1x11 checkerboard strip to the top edge, starting at the top right corner and stopping a few inches from the end of the strip. Press the stitched section of the seam only.

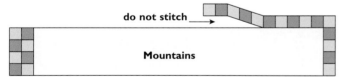

do not stitch →

Mountains

2. Sew embroidery background H to the right edge of the mountains unit and embroidery background I to the top right edge of the unit. Join a 1x7 checkerboard strip to the right edge and a 1x14 checkerboard strip to the top edge. Press after each addition. Add the four-block Pathways unit to the left edge of the top checkerboard section. Press. Then complete the seam across the top of the mountains unit.

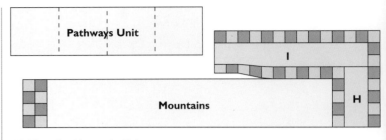

Making the Mountain Unit

3. Photocopy the pine bough embroidery patterns, sections 1–5 (pages 54–55), enlarging 200%. Trace section 1 (with two repeats) and section 2, matching the ends to make a large backwards L-shaped pattern. Transfer the design to pieces H and I of the mountains unit. Embroider in stem stitch, using the floss colors indicated on the pattern. Set the unit aside.

4. Stitch a 2x8 checkerboard strip to the bottom edge of the cabin block. Press. Stitch the J embroidery background pieces to the left and top edges, pressing after each addition. Join a 2x12 checkerboard strip to right edge. Transfer pine bough embroidery sections 1, 2, and 3 in mirror image to the L-shaped gold area. Embroider as in step 3.

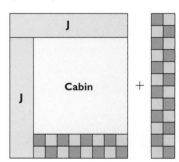

5. Join the Animal Tracks deer and squirrel blocks to the top and bottom edges of the single-fish unit. Press. Stitch a 1x14 checkerboard strip to each side edge. Press. Stitch a 1x8 checkerboard strip to the top and bottom edges. Press.

6. Stitch the 4" x 24" Flying Geese unit to the right edge of the cabin unit. Add the four-block Pine Bough Logs unit to the lower edge of the cabin unit, starting at the lower right corner and stopping a few inches before the lower left corner. Join the unit made in step 5 to the right edge. Press after each addition. Set the cabin unit aside.

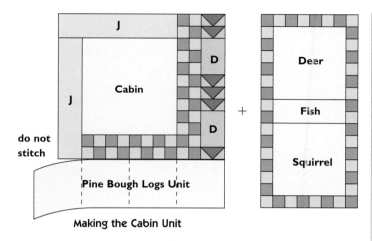

Making the Cabin Unit

do not stitch

7. Stitch a 1x6 checkerboard strip to the top and bottom edges of the Animal Tracks fish block. Press. Join the vertical Pine Tree unit and a 2x6 checkerboard unit to the lower edge, pressing after each addition. Set the unit aside.

8. Stitch the 4" x 16" Flying Geese unit to the lower edge of the five-fish unit, starting at the lower left corner and stopping a few inches before the end of the strip. Press. Stitch a 1x9 checkerboard strip to the right edge of embroidery background K. Press. Stitch a 1x4 checkerboard strip to the lower edge. Press. Stitch this unit to the left edge of the five-fish unit. Join the horizontal Pine Tree unit to the lower edge. Transfer pine bough embroidery section 5 to background strip K. Embroider as in steps 3 and 4. Set the five-fish unit aside.

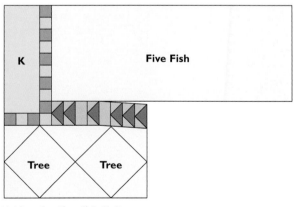

Making the Five-Fish Unit

9. Join the two Animal Tracks bear blocks to a 2x6 checkerboard strip so that the bears face each other. Press. Add the pinecones block to the right edge and embroidery background L to the lower edge, pressing after each addition. Transfer the pinecones embroidery design (page 55) to the middle of background L. Transfer pine bough embroidery sections 1 and 4 on each side of the pinecones in mirror image. Embroider and set aside.

10. Join all the units, stitching the seams in numbered order as shown on the quilt assembly diagram. The seams that were sewn partway will now be completed. Press each seam in the direction it wants to go.

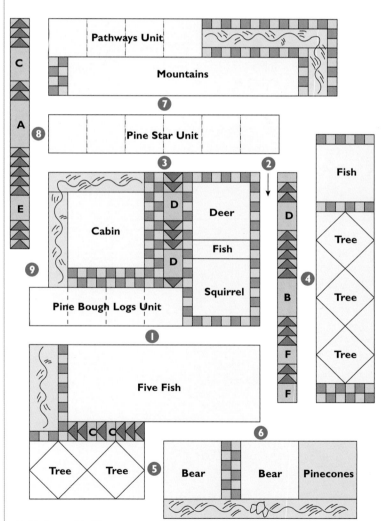

Quilt Assembly Diagram
Stitch the seams in the order shown

11. Add the side inner borders to the quilt. Press. Add the top and bottom inner borders. Press. Follow the same stitching and pressing sequence to add the middle and outer borders.

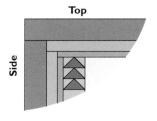

Border Corner Detail

12. Layer and finish the quilt. *Lakeside* uses a wide variety of machine-quilted designs to accentuate the sampler quality of the quilt. Some possibilities for you to try include cloudlike forms behind the mountains, outline-quilting around the various appliqué and patchwork shapes, and a boxy back-and-forth pattern in the checkerboard strips.

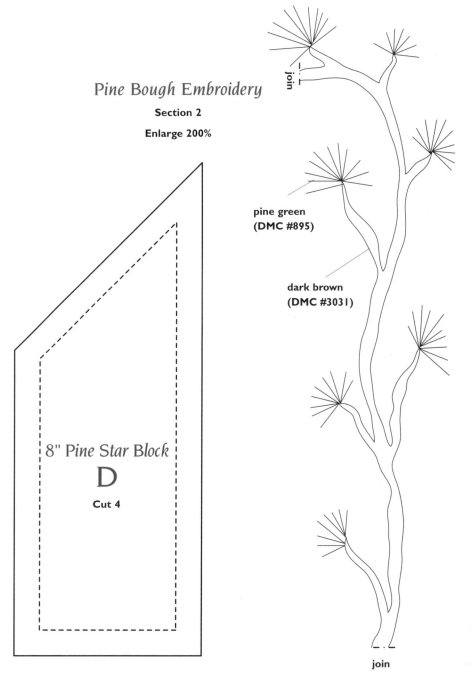

Pine Bough Embroidery

Section 2

Enlarge 200%

pine green
(DMC #895)

dark brown
(DMC #3031)

join

8" *Pine Star Block*

D

Cut 4

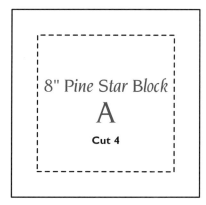

8" *Pine Star Block*

A

Cut 4

Lakeside Quilt

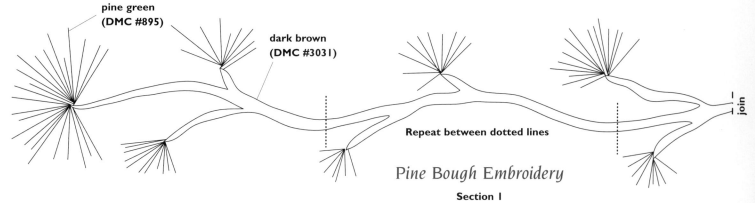

pine green
(DMC #895)

dark brown
(DMC #3031)

Repeat between dotted lines

join

Pine Bough Embroidery

Section I

Enlarge 200%

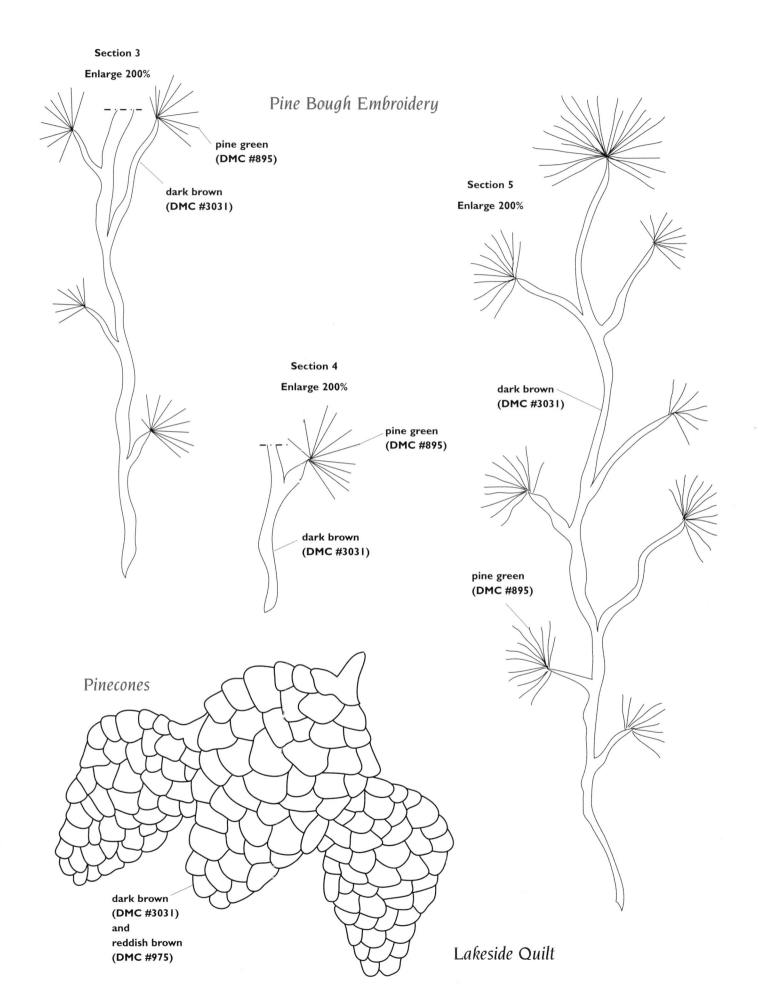

Section 3

Enlarge 200%

Pine Bough Embroidery

pine green
(DMC #895)

dark brown
(DMC #3031)

Section 5

Enlarge 200%

Section 4

Enlarge 200%

dark brown
(DMC #3031)

pine green
(DMC #895)

dark brown
(DMC #3031)

pine green
(DMC #895)

Pinecones

dark brown
(DMC #3031)
and
reddish brown
(DMC #975)

Lakeside Quilt

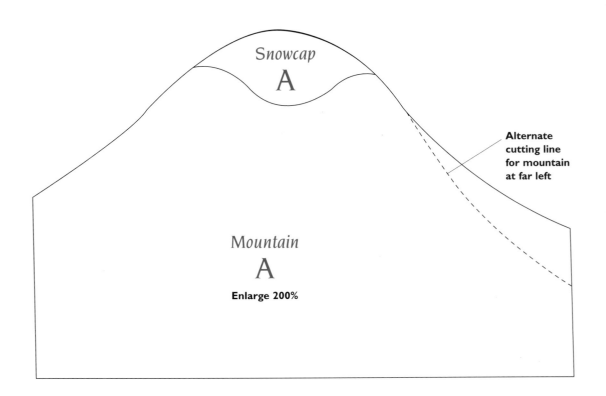

Snowcap
A

**Alternate
cutting line
for mountain
at far left**

Mountain
A

Enlarge 200%

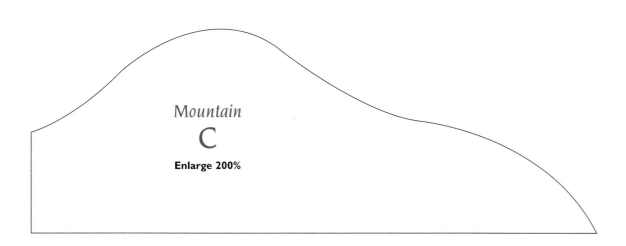

Mountain
C

Enlarge 200%

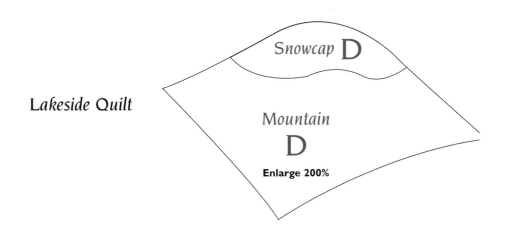

Lakeside Quilt

Snowcap D

Mountain
D

Enlarge 200%

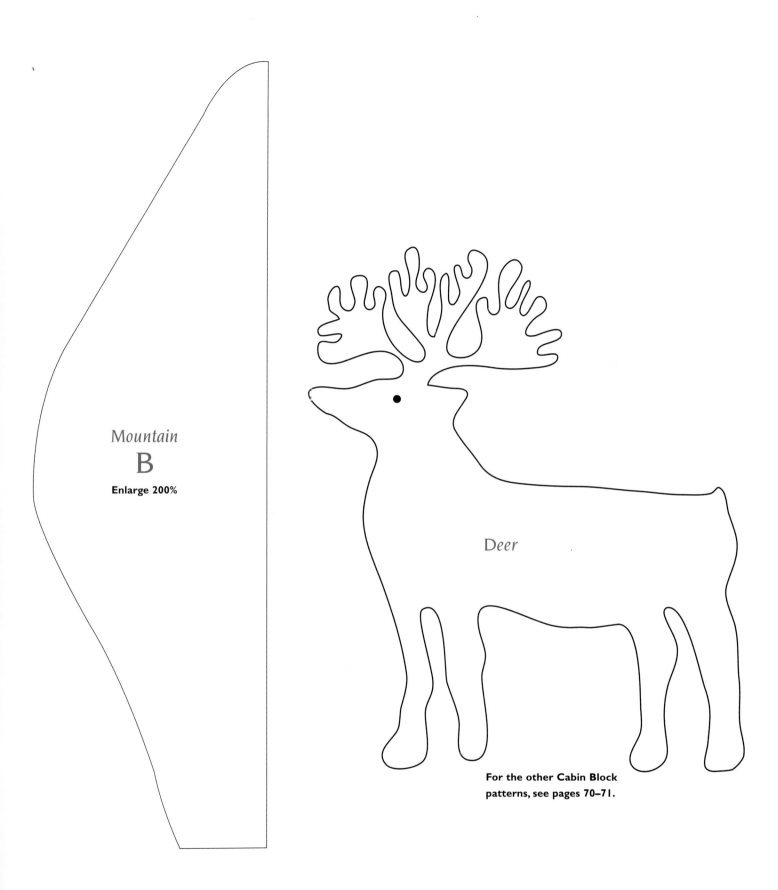

Mountain
B
Enlarge 200%

Deer

For the other Cabin Block
patterns, see pages 70–71.

Lakeside Quilt

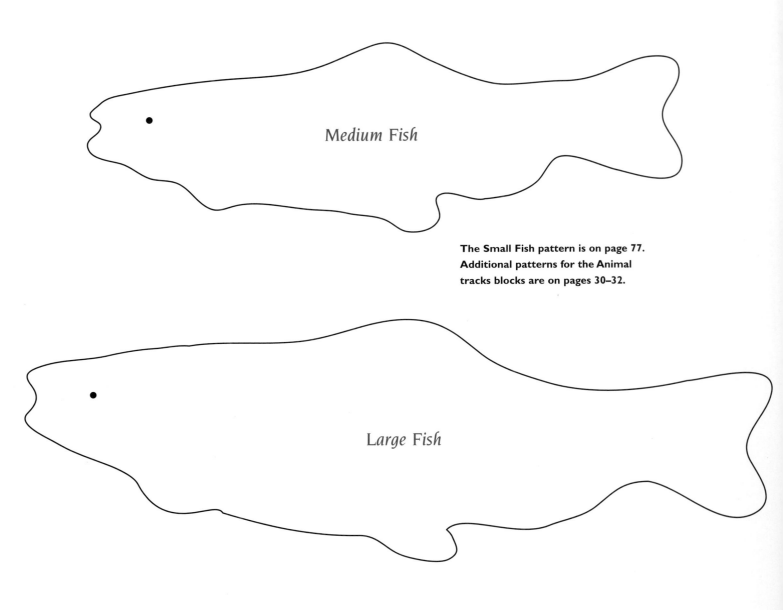

Medium Fish

The Small Fish pattern is on page 77. Additional patterns for the Animal tracks blocks are on pages 30–32.

Large Fish

Lakeside Quilt

Pine Bough Logs Quilt

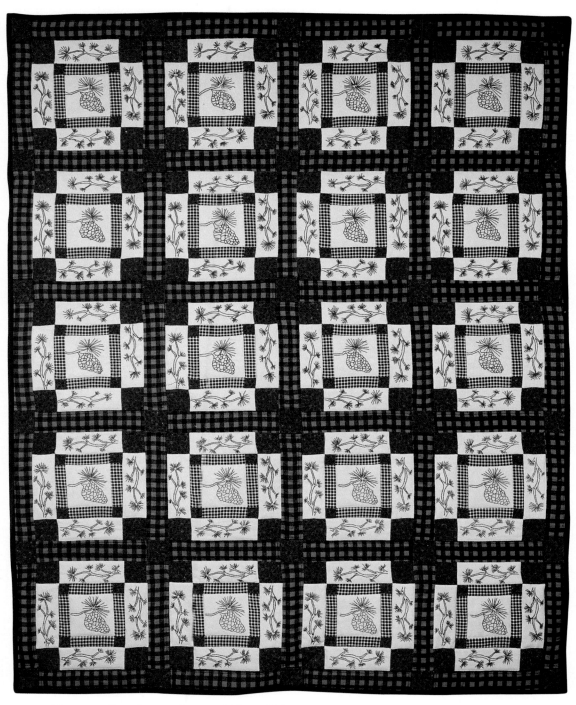

Designed by Jean Wells and Lawry Thorn; 50½" x 62½"

Bright blue and red flannels bring out the best in our embroidered pine boughs. The pinecones appear full and round in the summer, before gentle winds bring them to the ground or squirrels use them for a feast. The rich green color of the pine needles appears especially vibrant against the blue summer sky, a look we tried to capture with blue-checked sashing strips. There's lots of embroidery in this quilt, to help you while away the hours any time of year.

Materials

Flannel fabrics:

1⅝ yards cream for embroidery background

⅝ yard green check for Pine Bough Logs blocks

⅞ yard red for Pine Bough Logs blocks and sashing squares

1¼ yards blue-and-black check for sashing

⅜ yard for binding

3¾ yards backing

55" x 67" quilt batting

Embroidery floss:

dark brown (DMC #3031)

reddish brown (DMC #975)

pine green (DMC #895)

BASIC INSTRUCTIONS

Embroidery Design Transfer (page 12)

Stem Stitch (page 13)

Pine Bough Logs (page 16)

Finishing a Quilt (page 23)

Cutting

From the cream, cut three 4½" x 42" strips (A) and six 6½" x 42" strips (D); cut three of the D strips into forty 2½" x 6½" rectangles.

From the green check, cut six 1½" x 42" strips (B1) and two 4½" x 42" strips (B2).

From the red, cut four 1½" x 42" strips (C) and eight 2½" x 42" strips (E). Cut two of the E strips into thirty 2½" squares for the sashing.

From blue-and-black check, cut thirteen 2½" x 42" strips; cut into forty-nine 2½" x 10½" strips for the sashing.

Assembly

1. Stitch two B1 strips to each A strip, right sides together, using a ¼" seam allowance. Press toward the B fabric. Cut into twenty 4½" segments.

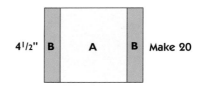

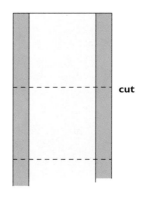

2. Stitch two C strips to each B2 strip. Press toward the B fabric. Cut into forty 1½" segments.

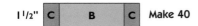

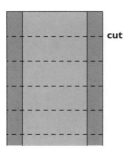

3. Join the segments from steps 1 and 2 to make 20 center units.

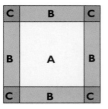

Make 20

4. Stitch two E strips to each D strip. Press toward the E fabric. Cut into forty 2½" segments.

Make 40

5. Stitch two D rectangles to opposite edges of each center unit. Stitch two EDE segments to the remaining edges to complete the block.

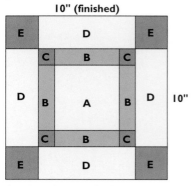

Pine Bough Logs Block
Make 20

6. Transfer the pinecone embroidery pattern to the cream square A at the center of each block. Transfer the pine bough pattern to each cream rectangle D. Make each block identical, positioning the pine boughs as shown in the closeup photograph below. Embroider the marked lines in stem stitch, using the floss colors indicated on the patterns. Alternate between dark brown and reddish brown floss when stitching the pinecones to make the individual petals stand out.

7. Sew a sashing strip to the left edge of each block. Join 4 block/sashing units together in a row. Add a fifth sashing strip to the right edge. Make 5 rows total.

8. Sew a red sashing square to each remaining sashing strip. Stitch 4 square/sashing units together, ending with a fifth red sashing square, to make a horizontal sashing strip. Make 6 strips total.

9. Join the block rows and horizontal sashing strips as shown in the quilt diagram.

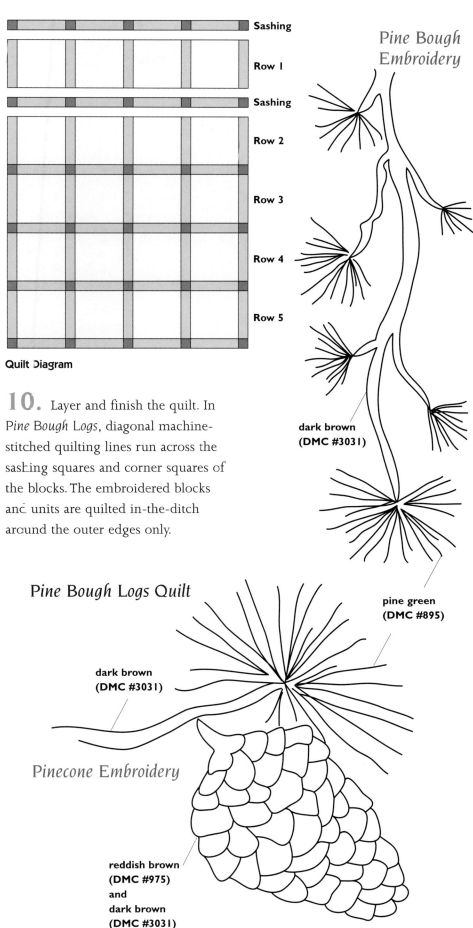

Sashing

Row 1

Sashing

Row 2

Row 3

Row 4

Row 5

Quilt Diagram

10. Layer and finish the quilt. In *Pine Bough Logs*, diagonal machine-stitched quilting lines run across the sashing squares and corner squares of the blocks. The embroidered blocks and units are quilted in-the-ditch around the outer edges only.

Pine Bough Embroidery

dark brown (DMC #3031)

pine green (DMC #895)

Pine Bough Logs Quilt

dark brown (DMC #3031)

Pinecone Embroidery

reddish brown (DMC #975) and dark brown (DMC #3031)

Animal Tracks Wall Hanging

Designed by Jean Wells and Lawry Thorn; 35" x 22"

Instead of piecing this Animal Tracks block, we appliquéd it. Trees and arrows complete the simple arrangement. You may want to add mountains, a cabin, or an animal or two to create your own picture memory of a special day or location. A walking stick found on a hike in the woods would make a rustic hanger.

Materials

Flannel fabrics:

¾ yard blue sky print for background

¼ yard medium red print for Animal Tracks appliqués

⅛ yard dark red print Animal Tracks appliqués

⅛ yard red-and-black small check Animal Tracks appliqués

¼ yard blue-and-black medium check for arrow appliqués

⅛ yard each three different green plaids for tree appliqués

Scraps of brown for trunk appliqués

⅜ yard black for binding and hanger tabs

¾ yard backing

Paper-backed fusible web

39" x 26" batting

Black embroidery floss (DMC #310)

BASIC INSTRUCTIONS

Buttonhole Stitch Appliqué (page 10)

Cutting

From the blue sky print, cut a 35" x 22" rectangle for the background.

Use the patterns on pages 63–65 to prepare the fusible appliqués: 4 medium red print and 4 dark red print squares (A), 16 red-and-black small-check triangles (B), 4 short and 2 long blue-and-black medium-check arrows (C) (extend the pattern 4" as indicated for the long arrows), 2 small trees, 1 medium tree, and 2 large trees (we used green plaids for the tree tiers and brown scraps for the trunks).

From the black flannel, cut three 1½" x 42" strips and sew together into one long strip for the binding. Also cut one 5" x 22½" strip for the tabs.

Assembly

1. Fold the blue sky print background piece in quarters and finger-press to mark the center. Lay the piece flat, right side up.

2. Referring to the project photograph (page 62) and appliqué diagram, place the A squares on the background on point, starting at the center and working out. Place the B triangles around the edges to complete the Animal Tracks block.

3. Place one long and two short C arrows 1" below the top edge, pointing left. Place the other three C arrows 1" above the bottom edge, pointing right. Arrange the trees so the tiers overlap. Fuse all the appliqués in place. Work buttonhole stitch around the edges with black floss.

4. Assemble and quilt the layers. We used echo quilting around the trees and a freestyle scallop in other areas to suggest clouds. Bind the edges with the black binding strip.

5. Fold the black tab strip in half lengthwise, right side in, and stitch the longer edges together. Press the seam open. Turn right side out, center the seam, and press again. Cut apart into three 7½" pieces. Fold each piece in half and stitch the short edges together to form a loop for hanging.

6. Turn the wall hanging facedown. Position the three tabs, evenly spaced, across the top edge so that 2" of the loop will show on the right side. Hand-sew in place.

Animal Tracks Appliqué Diagram

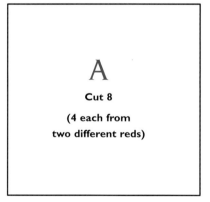

A

Cut 8

(4 each from
two different reds)

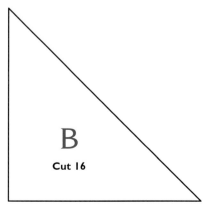

B

Cut 16

Animal Tracks Wall Hanging

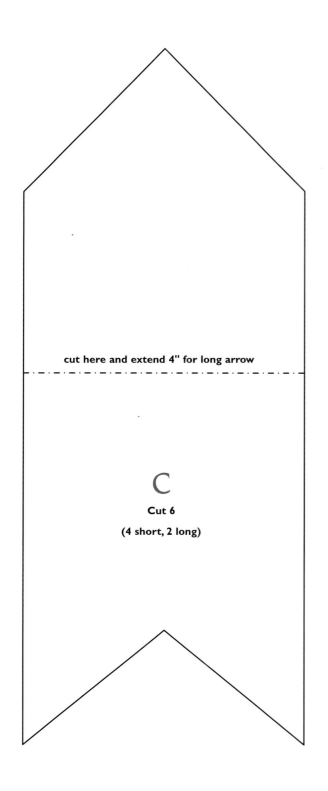

cut here and extend 4" for long arrow

C

Cut 6

(4 short, 2 long)

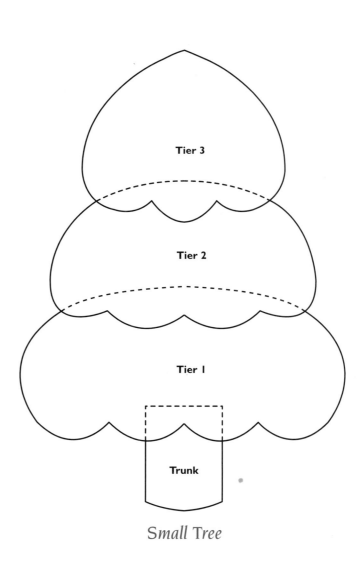

Tier 3

Tier 2

Tier 1

Trunk

Small Tree

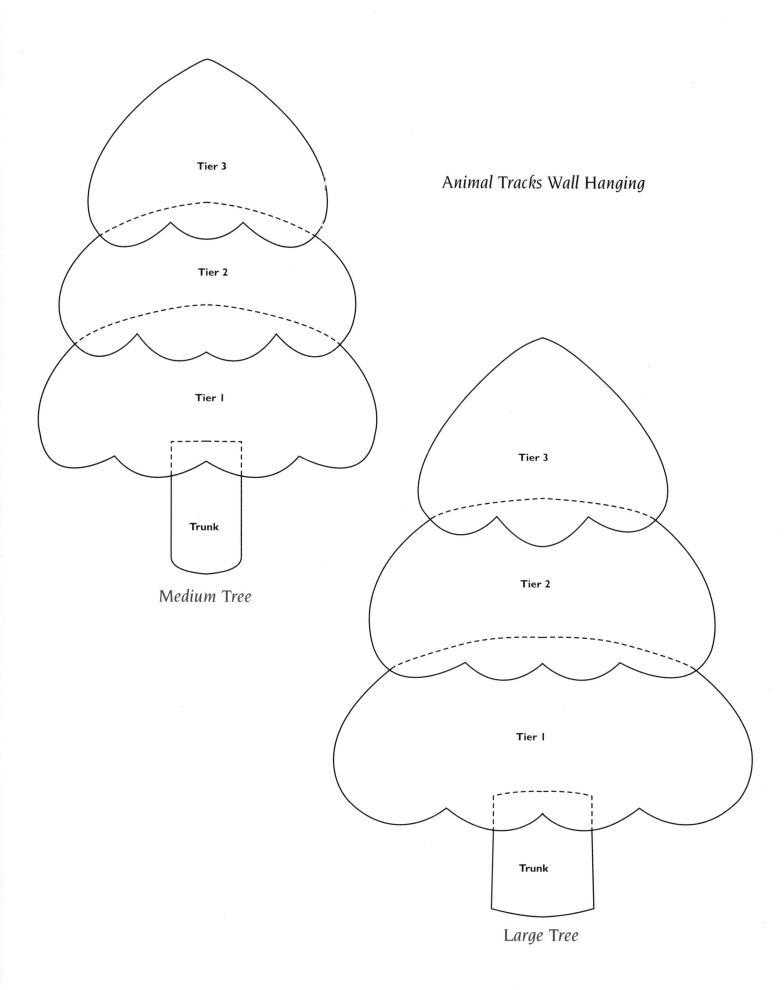

Tier 3

Tier 2

Tier 1

Trunk

Medium Tree

Animal Tracks Wall Hanging

Tier 3

Tier 2

Tier 1

Trunk

Large Tree

Appliquéd Pillowcases

Designed by Jean Wells and Lawry Thorn; 20" x 31"

Flannel pillowcases are cozy to sleep on and simple to sew. Buttonhole stitch appliqués (we used pine trees) give ordinary pillowcases a fun look for gifts, overnight guests, and special occasions. The pillowcase is sized to fit a standard 19" x 25" pillow but can easily be adapted for queen- and king-sized pillows. Just measure your pillows and make the needed adjustments. Follow our color palette or make up your own.

Materials

FOR ONE PILLOWCASE

Flannel fabrics:

$7/8$ yard red-and-black check for pillowcase

$3/8$ yard blue-and-white check for trim

Scrap of green plaid for tree appliqués

Paper-backed fusible web

Black embroidery floss (DMC #310)

BASIC INSTRUCTIONS

Buttonhole Stitch Appliqué (page 10)

Cutting

From the red-and-black check, cut one 28" x 41" rectangle for the pillowcase.

From the blue-and-white check, cut one 9" x 41" rectangle for the trim.

Use the pine tree pattern on page 77 to prepare 3 green plaid fusible appliqués.

Assembly

1. Fold the blue-and-white trim rectangle in half lengthwise, right side out, and press. Fold in half crosswise and finger-press. Open and lay flat, right side up. Center the three pine tree appliqués in the upper right quadrant, allowing for a ½" seam allowance at the top and right edges. Fuse the appliqués in place. Work buttonhole stitch in black floss around the edge of each appliqué.

2. Refold the trim piece on the lengthwise crease, right side out. Place the trim, appliqués facedown, on the right side of the pillowcase fabric, matching the raw edges. Stitch the long edges together using a ½" seam allowance. Serge or zigzag the seam allowance. Press the seam allowance toward the pillowcase.

3. Fold the pillowcase in half, right side in. Stitch the raw edges together with a ½" seam allowance; serge or zigzag the raw edges. Turn right side out and press. Work buttonhole stitch in black floss along the seam where the trim is joined to the pillowcase.

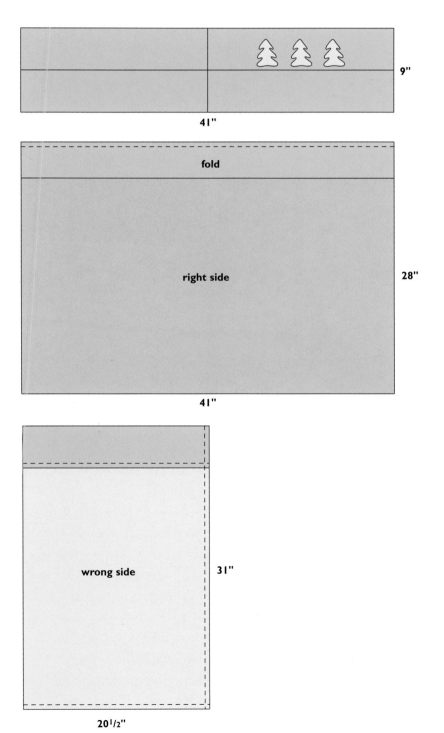

Lakeside Cabin Pillow

Designed by Jean Wells and Lawry Thorn; 20" x 20"

C reate this lakeside cabin scene using fusible flannel appliqués. Seek out rich green prints and plaids to create a woodsy atmosphere, and add a bright red door as a color complement. Bears cut from different grays add textural interest.

Materials

Flannel fabrics:

1 fat quarter (18" x 22") blue sky print for background

1 fat quarter (18" x 22") beige-and-white check for background

Assorted print, plaid, and solid scraps for appliqués (we used greens, golds, red, navy, gray, charcoal, and brown)

¾ yard blue-green check for border insert and backing

¼ yard red-and-black small check for border

¼ yard blue-and-white small check for border

Paper-backed fusible web

20" pillow form

Black embroidery floss (DMC #310)

BASIC INSTRUCTIONS

Buttonhole Stitch Appliqué (page 10)

Checkerboard Strips (page 14)

Finishing a Pillow (page 24)

Cutting

From the blue sky print, cut one 9" x 16½" rectangle for the background.

From the beige-and-white check, cut one 8" x 16½" rectangle for the background.

Use the patterns on pages 70–71 to prepare the fusible appliqués: 5 different green fir trees (three tiers each), 2 brown tree trunks, 1 brown cabin, 1 navy plaid roof, 1 gold print gable, 1 gray chimney, 4 gold print windows (2 large, 1 small, and 1 half-round), 1 red door, 1 gray plaid bear (reverse the pattern), 1 charcoal bear, 1 charcoal bear cub, and 3 navy plaid stepping stones.

From the blue-green check, cut four 1" x 16½" strips for the border inserts and two 14" x 20½" rectangles for the pillow back.

From the red-and-black check and the blue-and-white check, cut three 1½" x 42" strips each for the border.

Assembly

1. Place the two background rectangles right sides together. Stitch along one 16½" edge, using a ¼" seam allowance. Press the seam open.

2. Lay the background flat, right side up. Arrange the tree, cabin, bear, and stepping stone appliqués on top, overlapping them to create a woodland scene (see the photograph on page 68). Fuse in place, working from background to foreground.

3. Work buttonhole stitch in black floss around the edges of the appliqués. Embroider straight lines in stem stitch to define the cabin logs and windowpanes. Work a French knot for the doorknob and each animal eye.

4. Press each blue-green check insert strip in half lengthwise, right side out. Pin an insert strip to each side edge of the appliquéd unit, raw edges matching. Pin the two remaining insert strips to the top and bottom edges, so that the strips overlap at the corners.

5. Stitch the red-and-black and blue-and-white border strips together in pairs. Press. Cut into seventy-two 1½" segments. Join the segments together to make two 2x16 checkerboard strips for the side borders and two 2x20 checkerboard strips for the top and bottom borders, as shown in the pillow diagram.

6. Sew the side borders to the appliquéd unit. Press each seam allowance toward the border strip. Press again from the right side, so that the insert strip falls toward the inside. Sew the top and bottom borders and press in the same way.

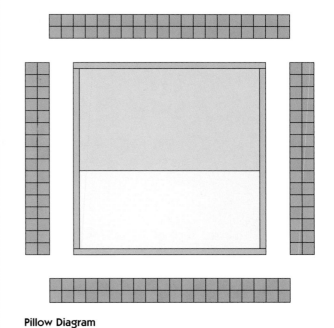

Pillow Diagram

7. Complete the pillow following the directions on page 24.

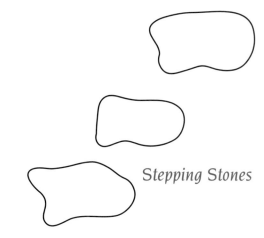

Stepping Stones

Lakeside Cabin Pillow

Use the patterns on these two pages to make the *Lakeside* quilt Cabin Block (page 48).

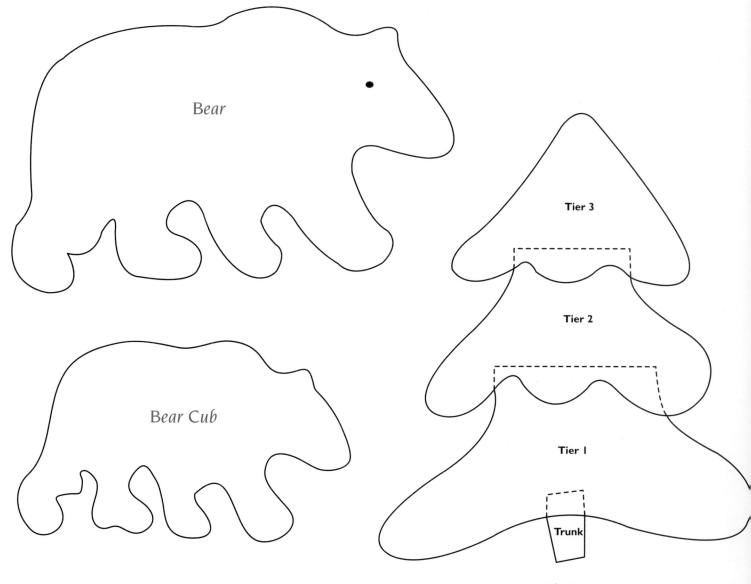

Bear

Bear Cub

Tier 3

Tier 2

Tier I

Trunk

Fir Tree

Lakeside Cabin Pillow

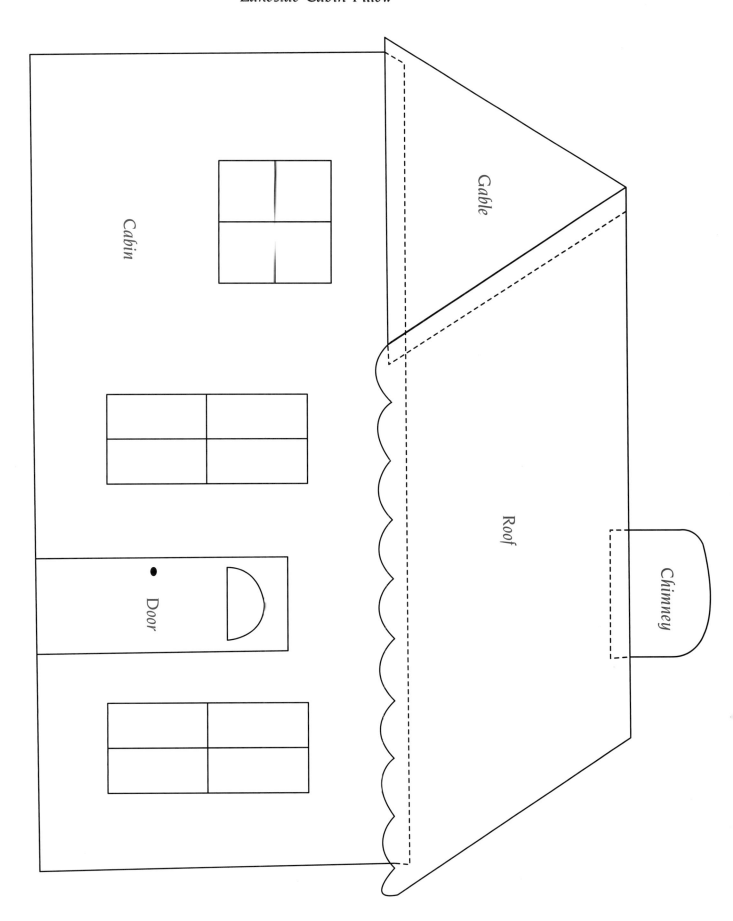

Cabin

Gable

Roof

Door

Chimney

FALL

Autumn Crazy-Patch Quilt

Designed by Jean Wells and Lawry Thorn; 54½" x 68½"

F all is an explosion of activity. Squirrels and other critters scurry about, gathering provisions for winter. Leaves swirl through the air, their many shades of yellow-green, rust, orange, and deep red landing in a crazy-patch on the ground. Combining these rich fall colors with appliqués and embroidery gave us the chance to show off some of our favorite stitches while capturing the season's riotous momentum.

Materials

1½ yards muslin for foundation piecing
Flannel fabrics:
  1⅜ yards light beige for center crazy-patch and sashing
  1¼ yards brown for crazy-patch and outer border
  ½ yard each of five coordinating colors for crazy-patch and outer border
  ¾ yard gray for crazy-patch and sashing squares
  ¾ yard black print for crazy-patch and inner border
  ¾ yard rust plaid for crazy-patch and outer border corners
  ¼ yard beige print for outer border
  ⅜ yard for binding
  3¼ yards backing
Paper-backed fusible web
59" x 73" batting
Embroidery floss:
  6 skeins dark brown (DMC #3031)
  2 skeins gold (DMC #977)
  5 more skeins in assorted colors; we included orange-rust (DMC #920), dark sage (DMC #3362), and black (DMC #310)

BASIC INSTRUCTIONS

Buttonhole Stitch Appliqué (page 10)
Embroidery Design Transfer (page 12)
Stem Stitch (page 13)
Herringbone Stitch (page 13)
Featherstitch (page 13)
Backstitch (page 13)
Four-Patch (page 14)
Flying Geese (page 18)
Finishing a Quilt (page 23)

Cutting

From the muslin, cut four 13½" x 42" strips; cut into twelve 13½" squares for foundation piecing.
Prepare crazy-patch templates 1–10 (pages 79–82), photocopying at 100%. Lay the light beige flannel right side up. Place Template 1 on top, line up a cutting ruler on the edge, and rotary-cut the shape. Transfer the block center mark to the shape (we did this by finger-creasing). Repeat to cut and mark 12 total. Stack the pieces. For the remaining patches, layer any three crazy-patch fabrics, right side up. Place templates 2–10 on top, pin in place, and cut out. Repeat twice, using each of the remaining crazy-patch fabrics, until you have enough pieces for 9 of the 12 blocks. Stack right side up by template number. The remaining pieces and appliqués will be fussy-cut in steps 4 and 8.
From the brown, cut five 4½" x 42" strips; cut into eighteen 4½" x 8½" rectangles for the outer border.
From the beige print and the assorted crazy-patch flannels (except brown), cut thirty-six 4½" squares for the outer border.

From the light beige, cut eleven 2½" x 42" strips; cut into thirty-one 2½" x 12½" strips for sashing.
From the gray, cut two 2½" x 42" strips; cut into twenty 2½" squares for sashing.
From the black print, cut six 1½" x 42" strips and sew into one long strip; cut two 58½" strips for the side inner borders and two 46½" strips for the top and bottom inner borders.
From the rust plaid, cut three 4½" x 42" strips; cut into four 4½" x 10½" rectangles for the side outer border corners and four 4½" x 11½" rectangles for the top and bottom outer border corners.

QUILTER'S TIP

Use flat-head pins when rotary-cutting. The pin head lies flat against the fabric, allowing your cutting ruler to rest firmly on top.

Assembly

1. Fold one muslin square in quarters to find the center, and finger-press to set the creases. Unfold the square and lay it flat. Place a light beige center patch right side up on the muslin, aligning the crease marks on both pieces.

2. Take one patch from stack #2. Position it right side up on the muslin square, referring to the block diagram and comparing the arrows on the templates to make sure the pieces are correctly oriented. When you are satisfied, turn Patch 2 face-down on the center patch and line up the edges to be joined. Machine-stitch ¼" from the edges through three layers of fabric. Flip Patch 2 right side up and press from the right side, concealing the seam allowance.

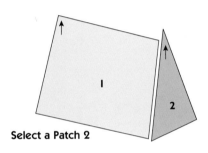

Select a Patch 2

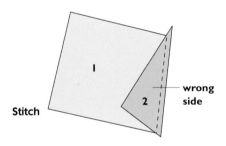

Stitch

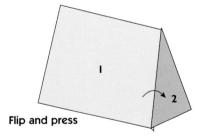

Flip and press

3. Repeat the step 2 method to select and add Patch 3. Continue in this manner, adding Patch 4, Patch 5, and so forth, until ten patches are used and the entire muslin square is covered. Square up the block to 12½".

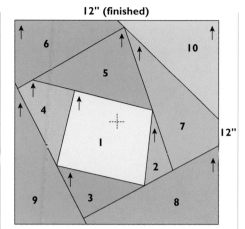

12" (finished)

12"

Crazy-Patch Block Diagram

4. Repeat steps 1–3 to make twelve crazy-patch blocks. Fussy-cut additional patches as needed, so that each block is different and the blocks contain a variety of color and textural contrasts.

5. Arrange the blocks in 4 rows. Rotate the blocks to vary the orientation of the center patch. Number each block lightly on the back and on the quilt diagram (page 76) for future reference.

QUILTER'S TIP

To encourage a random color selection, work on three or four blocks at a time. Lay out the blocks, pick the top patch from your stack, and assign it to one of the blocks. When none of the available colors seem to work and you feel stuck, fussy-cut a new patch.

6. Refer to the quilt photograph (page 73) to plan which embroidery and appliqué designs you'd like to use and to decide on their placement. For example, Block 1 at the top left features pinecone embroidery in the center patch and a fish appliqué in

Patch 7. Note also that you can combine two appliqués, such as the bear and pine tree in the center patch of Block 7. Jot down your ideas on the quilt diagram; you can always improvise as you go along.

7. Transfer the chickadee, pinecone, and pine bough embroidery patterns (page 78) to the patches you identified in step 6. Embroider the marked lines in stem stitch. Use the floss colors indicated on the patterns to embroider the center patches, but use any contrasting color to embroider darker-color patches.

8. Trace the bear cub, small fish, bunny, squirrel, chipmunk, deer, and pine tree patterns (page 77) onto fusible web, making one tracing for each appliqué desired. Cut the pieces apart, fuse them to the leftover crazy-patch fabrics, and cut out. Fuse the appliqués to the quilt blocks. Work buttonhole stitch around each appliqué, using contrasting floss.

9. Finish each block by embroidering decorative stitches, such as herringbone stitch and featherstitch, over some of the seams. Use a variety of floss colors.

10. Use the brown 4½" x 8½" rectangles and assorted 4½" squares to make 18 double half-square triangles.

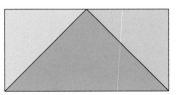

Make 18 assorted

11. Transfer the short twig embroidery design (page 78) to each brown triangle. Transfer the long twig design (page 78) to each sashing strip. Work the embroidery in stem stitch, using gold floss on the triangles and dark brown floss on the sashing strips.

12. Sew a sashing strip to the left edge of each block. Join 3 block/ sashing units together in a row. Add a fourth sashing strip to the right edge. Make 4 rows total.

13. Sew a sashing square to each remaining sashing strip. Stitch three of these units together, and finish with a fourth sashing square for a horizontal sashing strip. Make 5 strips total.

14. Join the block rows and horizontal sashing strips as shown. Add the side inner borders. Press. Add the top and bottom inner borders. Press.

15. For each side outer border, stitch 5 embroidered triangle units together; add a $4\frac{1}{2}$" x $10\frac{1}{2}$" corner piece to each end. For the top and bottom outer borders, stitch 4 embroidered triangle units together; add a $4\frac{1}{2}$" x $11\frac{1}{2}$" corner piece to each end. Add the side outer borders to the quilt. Press. Add the top and bottom outer borders. Press.

16. Layer and finish the quilt. In-the-ditch quilting around each block helps stabilize the layers of *Autumn Crazy-Patch*. The animal appliqués and embroidered designs are outline-quilted, causing them to puff out slightly.

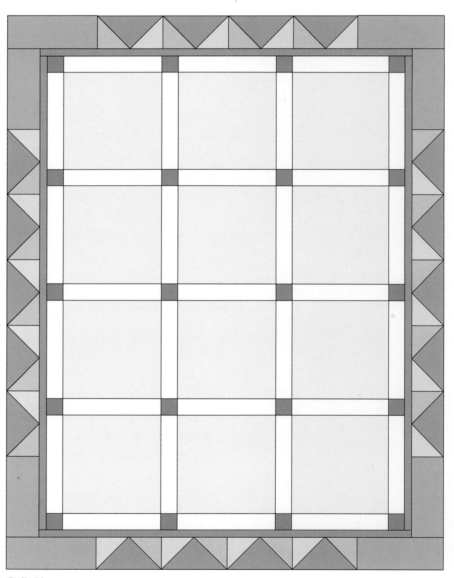

Quilt Diagram

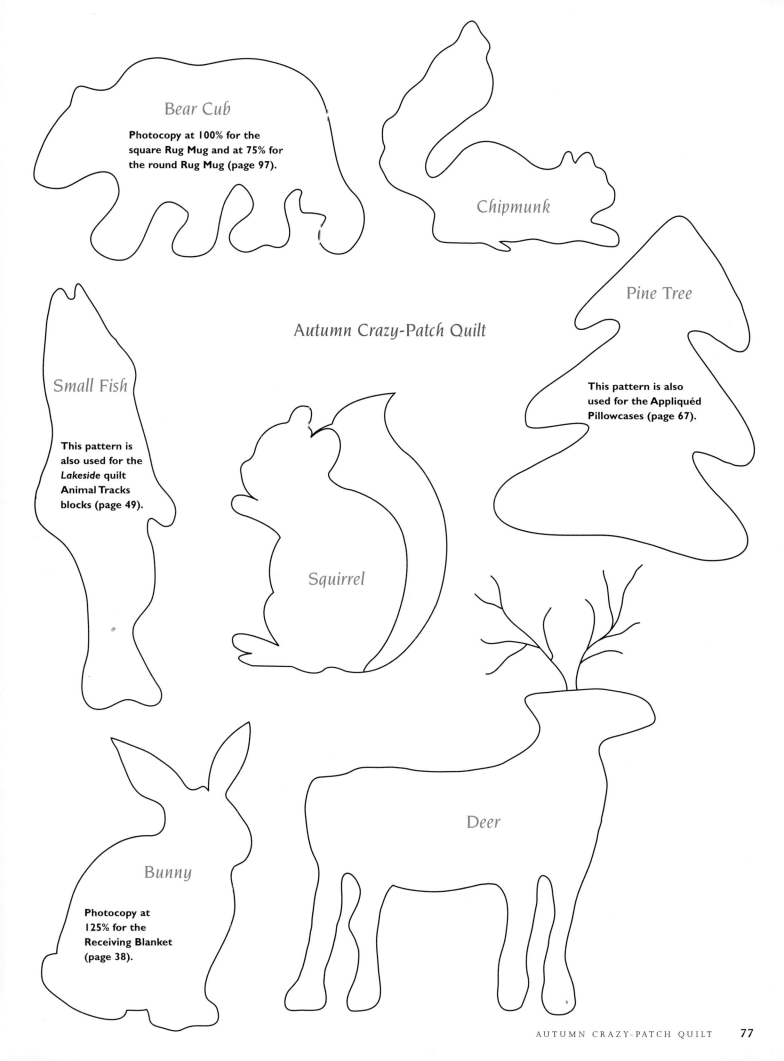

Bear Cub

Photocopy at 100% for the square Rug Mug and at 75% for the round Rug Mug (page 97).

Chipmunk

Pine Tree

Autumn Crazy-Patch Quilt

Small Fish

This pattern is also used for the Appliqued Pillowcases (page 67).

This pattern is also used for the *Lakeside* quilt Animal Tracks blocks (page 49).

Squirrel

Deer

Bunny

Photocopy at 125% for the Receiving Blanket (page 38).

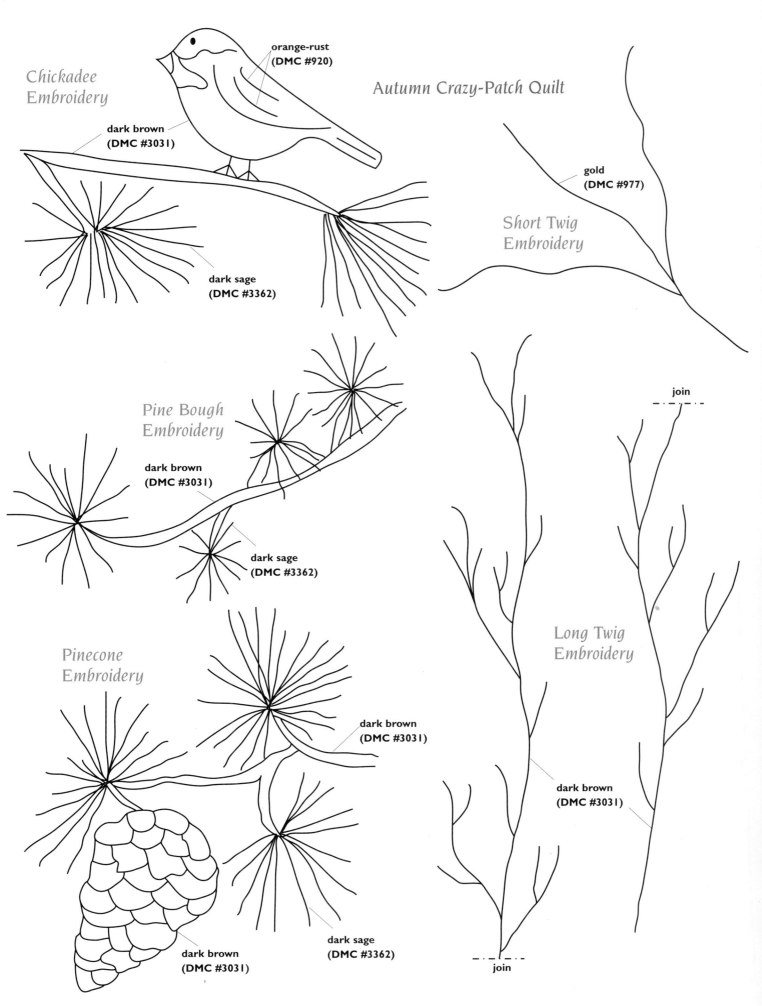

Chickadee Embroidery

orange-rust
(DMC #920)

Autumn Crazy-Patch Quilt

dark brown
(DMC #3031)

dark sage
(DMC #3362)

gold
(DMC #977)

Short Twig Embroidery

Pine Bough Embroidery

dark brown
(DMC #3031)

dark sage
(DMC #3362)

join

Long Twig Embroidery

Pinecone Embroidery

dark brown
(DMC #3031)

dark brown
(DMC #3031)

dark sage
(DMC #3362)

dark brown
(DMC #3031)

join

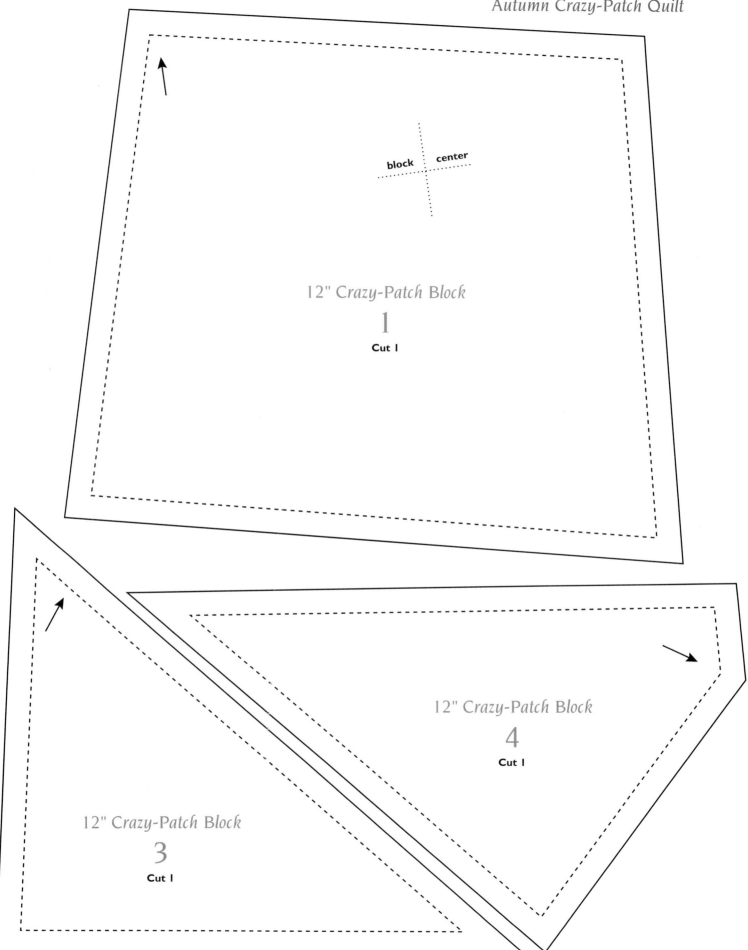

block center

12" Crazy-Patch Block

1

Cut 1

12" Crazy-Patch Block

4

Cut 1

12" Crazy-Patch Block

3

Cut 1

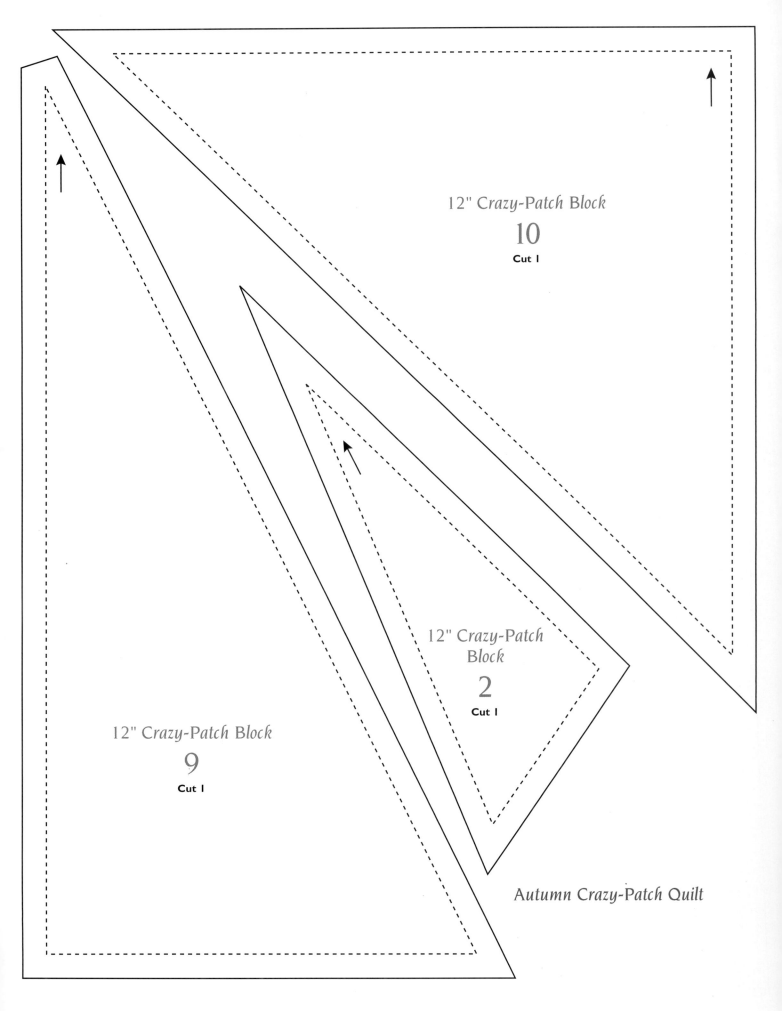

12" Crazy-Patch Block
10
Cut 1

12" Crazy-Patch
Block
2
Cut 1

12" Crazy-Patch Block
9
Cut 1

Autumn Crazy-Patch Quilt

Autumn Crazy-Patch Quilt

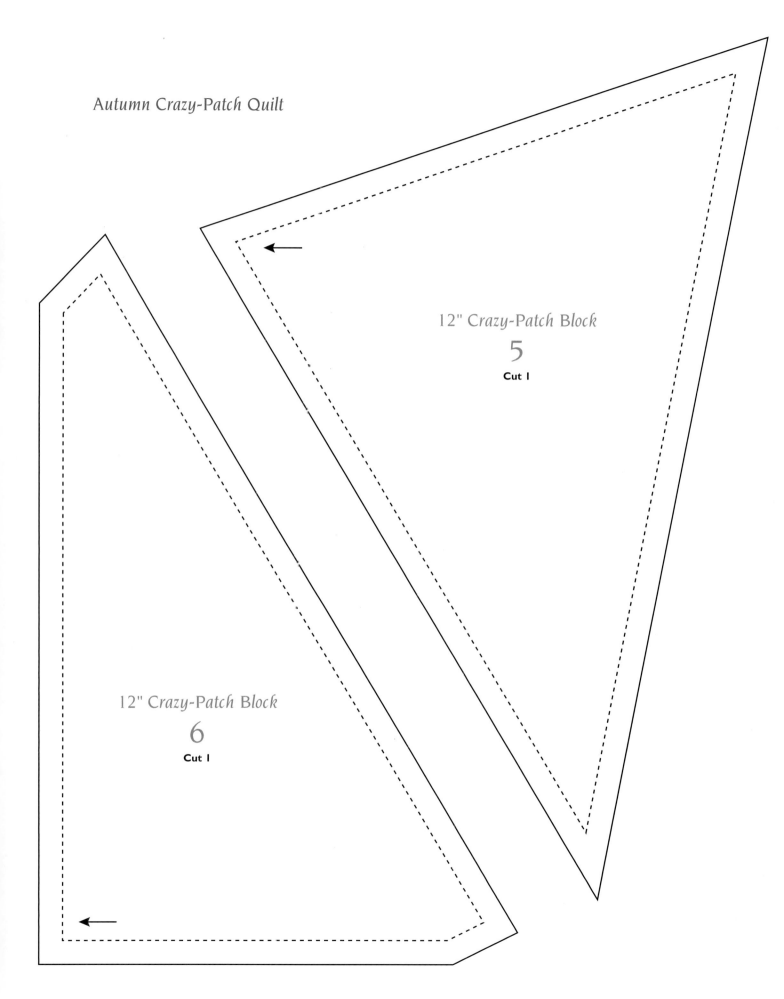

12" Crazy-Patch Block
5
Cut 1

12" Crazy-Patch Block
6
Cut 1

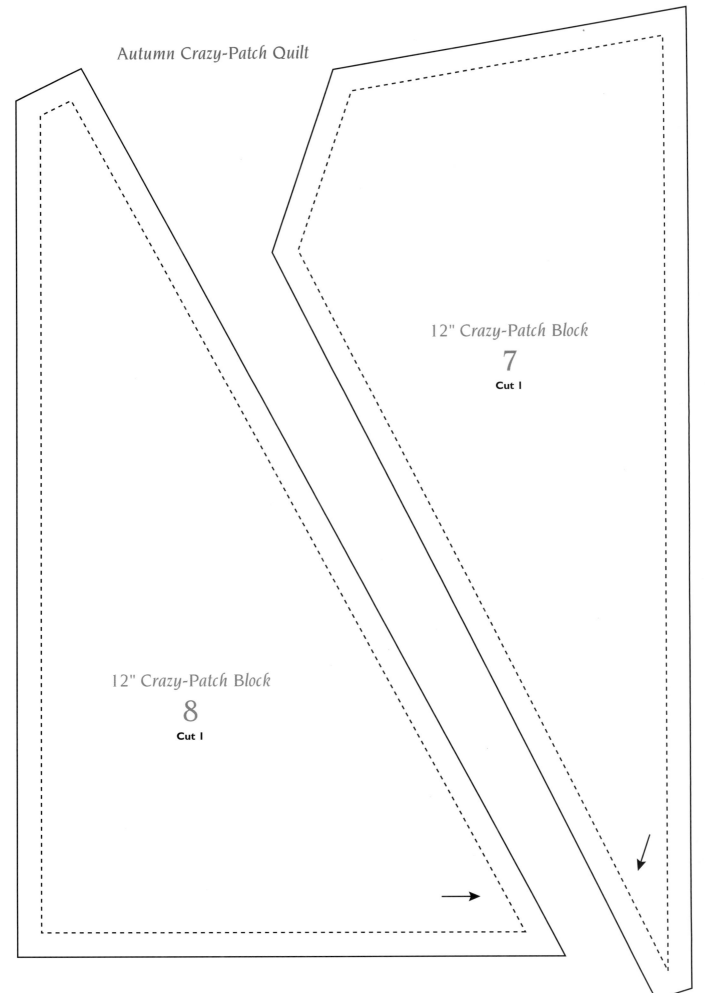

Autumn Crazy-Patch Quilt

12" Crazy-Patch Block

7

Cut 1

12" Crazy-Patch Block

8

Cut 1

Designed by Jean Wells and Lawry Thorn; 64½" x 81"

The colors in *Ponderosa Pines* remind us of the cooling fall weather we experience in Sisters, Oregon. Cooler nights first arrive in late August, and week by week, small but perceptible drops in the temperature let us know winter is approaching. Row by row, this quilt forecasts changes in the weather through rich fall colors, snowy white backgrounds, and dark strips that represent the long nights of winter.

Materials

Flannel fabrics:

$\frac{1}{2}$ yard black solid for checkerboard strips

$\frac{1}{2}$ yard gold plaid for checkerboard strips

$2\frac{1}{2}$ yards white for backgrounds

$\frac{1}{4}$ yard each of three different plaids for Four-Patch, Nine-Patch, and double half-square triangles

$\frac{1}{8}$ yard dark plaid for Four-Patch, Nine-Patch, and Friendship Stars

$\frac{1}{4}$ yard rust plaid for Four-Patch, Nine-Patch, and half-square triangles

$\frac{1}{2}$ yard green mini plaid for Four-Patch, Nine-Patch, half-square triangles, and trees

$\frac{1}{4}$ yard dark green plaid for Four-Patch, Nine-Patch, and trees

$\frac{5}{8}$ yard brown for double half-square triangles and tree trunks

$\frac{1}{4}$ yard each of two different yellow-gold prints for double half-square triangles

$1\frac{7}{8}$ yards black print for sashing and binding

$4\frac{3}{4}$ yards backing

69" x 85" batting

Embroidery floss:

dark brown (DMC #3031)

dark sage (DMC #3362)

BASIC INSTRUCTIONS

Embroidery Design Transfer (page 12)

Stem Stitch (page 13)

Four-Patch (page 14)

Checkerboard Strips (page 14)

Nine-Patch (page 15)

Half-Square Triangles (page 18)

Friendship Star (page 19)

Pine Tree (page 22)

Finishing a Quilt (page 23)

Cutting

CHECKERBOARD ROWS

From the black solid, cut six $2\frac{1}{2}$" x 42" strips.

From the gold plaid, cut six $2\frac{1}{2}$" x 42" strips.

FOUR-PATCH ROW

From the white, cut one $8\frac{1}{2}$" x $26\frac{1}{2}$" rectangle for the pine bough embroidery, four $2\frac{3}{8}$" x $13\frac{1}{4}$" strips, and two $6\frac{3}{4}$" x $8\frac{1}{2}$" rectangles. Cut two $5\frac{1}{2}$" squares; cut into 8 quarter-square triangles. Cut four 3" squares; cut into 8 half-square triangles.

From the various plaids, cut a total of twenty-four 2" squares. (If you prefer, cut these pieces later from the scraps.)

NINE-PATCH ROW

From the various plaids, cut eight different 2" x 21" strips; cut into eighty-one 2" squares.

From the white, cut two $3\frac{7}{8}$" x 7" rectangles. Cut four $7\frac{3}{4}$" squares; cut into 16 quarter-square triangles. Cut two $4\frac{1}{8}$" squares; cut into 4 half-square triangles.

DOUBLE HALF-SQUARE TRIANGLES ROWS

From the brown, cut four $4\frac{1}{2}$" x 42" strips; cut into sixteen $4\frac{1}{2}$" x $8\frac{1}{2}$" rectangles.

From the yellow-gold prints and plaids, cut a total of thirty-two $4\frac{1}{2}$" squares.

FRIENDSHIP STARS ROW

For the Blocks:

From the various plaids, cut twenty-eight $1\frac{1}{2}$" squares. From the dark plaid, cut fourteen $2\frac{7}{8}$" squares; cut into 28 half-square triangles for the star points.

From the white, cut twenty-eight $2\frac{1}{2}$" squares and fourteen $2\frac{7}{8}$" squares; cut the larger white squares into 28 half-square triangles.

For the Background:

From the white, cut one $10\frac{1}{4}$" x 42" strip; cut into three $10\frac{1}{4}$" squares; cut diagonally in both directions for 12 quarter-square triangles. Cut two $5\frac{3}{8}$" squares; cut in half diagonally for 4 half-square triangles. Cut two $2\frac{3}{4}$" x 9" rectangles.

HALF-SQUARE TRIANGLES ROW

From the rust and green mini plaids, cut one $4\frac{7}{8}$" x 42" strip each. Place both strips right sides together. Cut into eight $4\frac{7}{8}$" squares; then cut diagonally into half-square triangles. Do not separate the pairs; they are now ready for sewing.

PINE TREES ROW

For the Blocks:

Prepare templates A through H (pages 88–89), photocopying at 100%. Cut 3 sets of A, B, and C from the green mini plaid and 2 sets from the green plaid. From the brown solid, cut 10 each (reverse 5) of D and E. From the white, cut 10 each (reverse 5) of F, G, and H.

For the Background:

From the white, cut two $12\frac{3}{4}$" x 42" strips; cut into four $12\frac{3}{4}$" squares; cut diagonally in both directions for 16 quarter-square triangles. Cut two $6\frac{5}{8}$" squares; cut in half diagonally for 4 half-square triangles. Cut two $3\frac{3}{4}$" x 12" rectangles.

SASHING

From the black print, cut seventeen $2\frac{1}{2}$" x 42" strips and sew together into one long strip; cut eleven $64\frac{1}{2}$" strips for the horizontal sashing. Set aside the remainder for the binding.

Assembly

1. **Checkerboard Rows.** Sew the black and gold plaid strips together in pairs. Cut into ninety-six $2\frac{1}{2}$" segments. Join the segments to make three 2x32 checkerboard strips.

2. **Four-Patch Row.** Photocopy the pine bough half-pattern (page 87), enlarging it 135% and reversing the image to complete the pattern. Transfer the design to the $8\frac{1}{2}$" x $26\frac{1}{2}$" white rectangle. Embroider the design in stem stitch, using the floss colors indicated on the pattern.

3. Piece the 24 assorted plaid 2" squares together at random to make 6 Four-Patch units.

Make 6 assorted

4. Place 3 Four-Patch units side by side on point. Fill in with 4 white quarter-square triangles and 4 white half-square triangles at the corners. Join the pieces in diagonal rows. Join the rows together, adding the two single corner triangles last. Repeat.

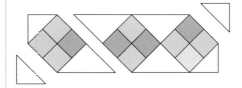

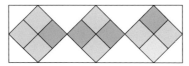

Make 2

5. Stitch two $2\frac{3}{8}$" x $13\frac{1}{4}$" white strips to each Four-Patch unit. Press. Add a $6\frac{3}{4}$" x $8\frac{1}{2}$" white rectangle to one end. Press. Join the pieced units to each end of the embroidered rectangle. Press.

6. **Nine-Patch Row.** Piece the 81 assorted plaid 2" squares together at random to make 9 Nine-Patch units.

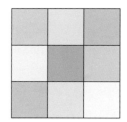

Make 9 assorted

7. Place the Nine-Patch units side by side on point. Fill in with 8 white quarter-square triangles and 4 white half-square triangles at the corners. Join the pieces in diagonal rows. Press. Join the rows together, adding the two single corner triangles last. Press. Stitch the $3\frac{7}{8}$" x 7" white rectangles to each end. Press. Trim the unit to 7" x $64\frac{1}{2}$".

8. **Double Half-Square Triangles Rows.** Use the brown $4\frac{1}{2}$" x $8\frac{1}{2}$" rectangles and the yellow-gold print and plaid $4\frac{1}{2}$" squares to make 16 double half-square triangles. Photocopy the short twig pattern (page 78). Transfer the design to each brown triangle. Embroider the twig in stem stitch using gold floss. Stitch 8 "twig" units together and press to complete a double half-square triangles row. Make 2 rows.

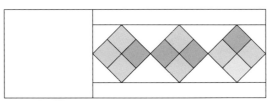

Making the Four-Patch Row

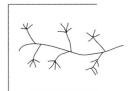

+

9. Friendship Stars Row. Piece the 28 assorted plaid 1½" squares together at random to make 7 Four-Patch units. Stitch the white and dark plaid half-square triangles together in pairs to make 28 star point units. For each block, join 1 Four-Patch unit, 4 star point units, and 4 white 2½" squares. Repeat to make 7 Friendship Star blocks.

6" (finished)

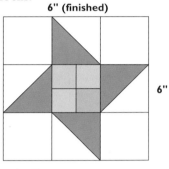

6"

Make 7

10. Place the Friendship Star blocks side by side on point. Fill in with 12 white quarter-square triangles and 4 white half-square triangles at the corners. Join the pieces in diagonal rows. Join the rows together, adding the two single corner triangles last. Press. Stitch a 2¾" x 9" white rectangle to each end. Press. Trim the unit to 9" x 64½".

11. Half-Square Triangles Row. Stitch the half-square triangles together along the diagonal as paired. Press open. Join the units together in a single strip, making sure all the diagonal seams face in the same direction. Press.

12. Pine Trees Row. Join pieces A through H to make 3 green mini plaid and 2 green plaid Pine Tree blocks.

8" (finished)

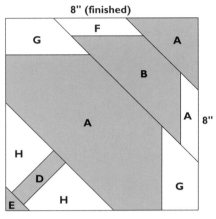

8"

Make 3 green mini plaid and 2 green plaid

13. Place the Pine Tree blocks side by side on point, alternating the colors. Fill in with 8 white quarter-square triangles and 4 white half-square triangles at the corners. Join the pieces in diagonal rows. Join the rows together, adding the two single corner triangles last. Press. Stitch a 3¾" x 12" white rectangle to each end. Press. Trim the unit to 12" x 64½".

14. Lay out the 10 pieced rows and 11 sashing strips alternately, referring to the quilt photograph (page 83) and quilt diagram. Join the pieced rows and sashing together. Press toward the sashing.

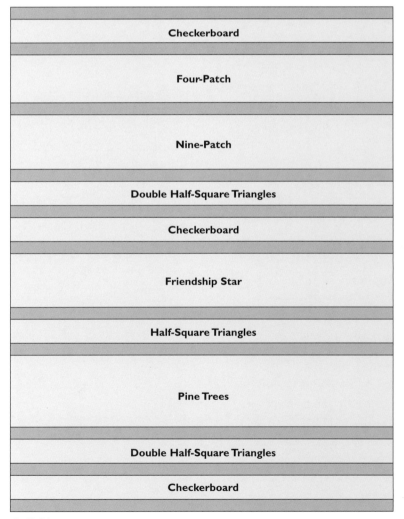

Quilt Diagram

15. Layer and finish the quilt. In-the-ditch stitching defines the strong horizontal lines of *Ponderosa Pines* while stabilizing the quilt layers. A simple swirl shape, stitched freestyle in the light areas behind the Pine Star blocks, suggests a gently blowing wind. Outline quilting echoes outward from the pine bough embroidery, and inward on the patchwork shapes. Leaf shapes were added alongside the trees.

QUILTER'S TIP

To join long strips accurately, mark the midpoint of each long edge with a pin. Place the strips right sides together, matching the midpoints and ends, and pin at all three spots. Add four more pins evenly spaced in between to prevent the fabric from shifting and stretching as you sew.

Pine Bough Embroidery

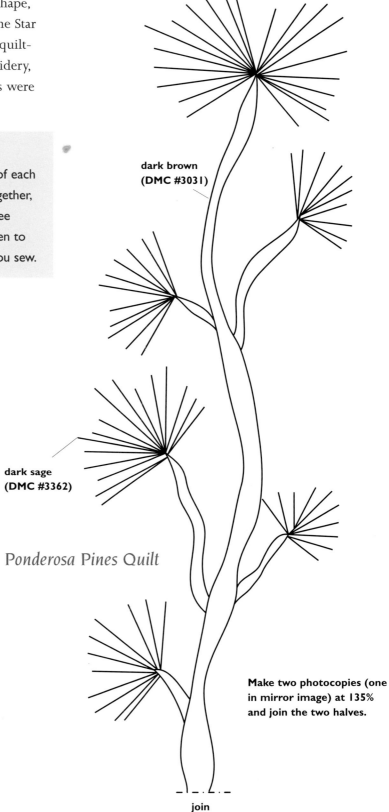

dark brown
(DMC #3031)

dark sage
(DMC #3362)

Ponderosa Pines Quilt

Make two photocopies (one in mirror image) at 135% and join the two halves.

join

Ponderosa Pines Quilt

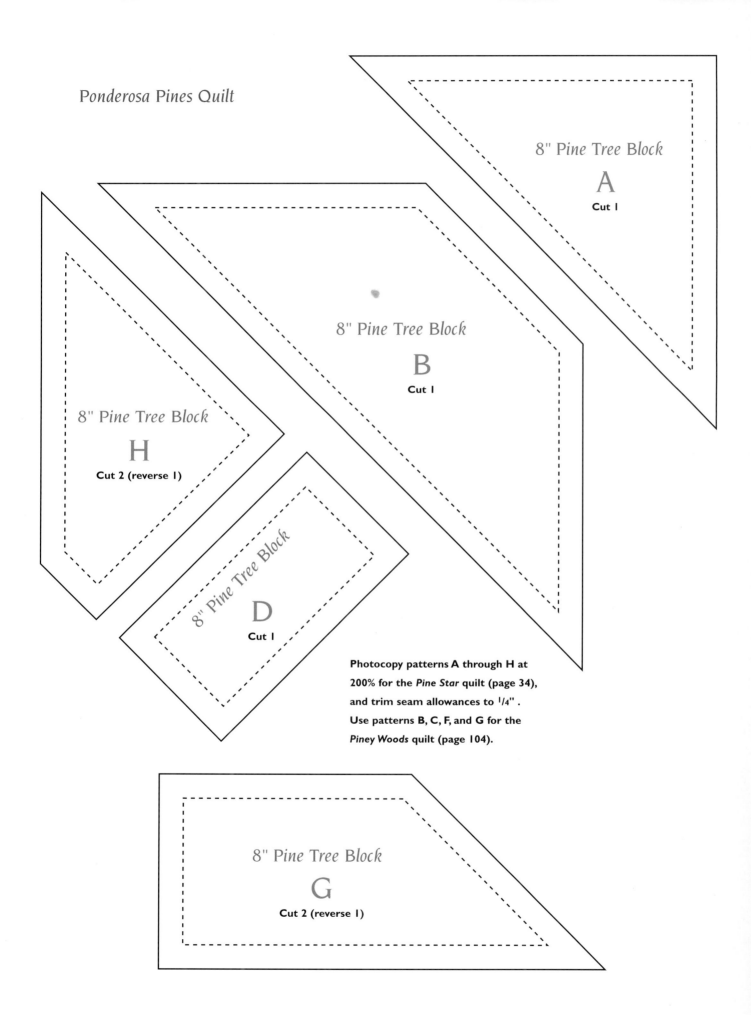

8" Pine Tree Block

A

Cut 1

8" Pine Tree Block

B

Cut 1

8" Pine Tree Block

H

Cut 2 (reverse 1)

8" Pine Tree Block

D

Cut 1

Photocopy patterns A through H at 200% for the *Pine Star* quilt (page 34), and trim seam allowances to 1/4" . Use patterns B, C, F, and G for the *Piney Woods* quilt (page 104).

8" Pine Tree Block

G

Cut 2 (reverse 1)

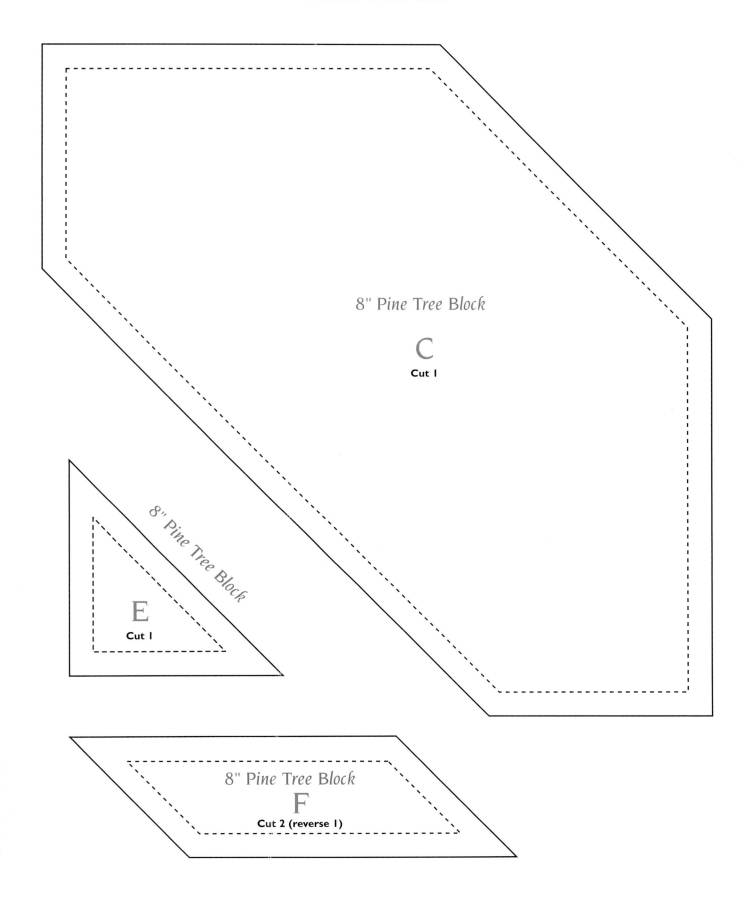

8" Pine Tree Block

C

Cut 1

8" Pine Tree Block

E

Cut 1

8" Pine Tree Block

F

Cut 2 (reverse 1)

Autumn Mountains Pillow

Designed by Jean Wells and Lawry Thorn; 18" x 11"

A mountain scene is flanked by two crazy-patch panels in this small pillow. Pay special attention to the flannels you choose for the mountain appliqués. Distant mountains in purple, foreground mountains in green, and middle mountains in browns and golds help create a realistic scene.

Materials

Flannel fabrics:

¼ yard yellow tan for mountains background

Ten assorted prints and plaids, at least 6" x 12" each, for mountains and crazy-patch (we used purples, browns, rust, and greens)

⅜ yard olive green for borders and backing

Scrap of muslin for foundation piecing

Paper-backed fusible web

Black embroidery floss (DMC #310)

Fiberfill

BASIC INSTRUCTIONS

Buttonhole Stitch Appliqué (page 10)

Cutting

From the yellow tan, cut one 6" x 11½" rectangle for the mountains background.

Use mountain patterns 1–8 (page 92) to prepare the fusible appliqués: mountains 1, 2, and 3 in purples, mountains 4, 5, and 6 in browns and rust, and mountains 7 and 8 in greens.

From the muslin, cut two 2½" x 6" rectangles for foundation piecing.

Prepare crazy-patch templates 1–6 (page 93), photocopying at 100%. For each template, choose a different print or plaid and cut 2 patches (reverse 1).

From the olive green, cut two 2" x 6" strips for the side borders, two 2" x 18½" strips for the top and bottom borders, and one 11½" x 18½" rectangle for the pillow back.

Assembly

1. Lay the 6" x 11½" yellow-tan background piece right side up. Arrange mountain appliqués 1–8 on top, overlapping them as shown in the assembly diagram (page 92). Fuse in place in numbered order. Work buttonhole stitch in black floss around all the exposed edges.

2. Lay one muslin rectangle flat. Position crazy-patch 1, right side up, on the lower right corner. Place crazy-patch 2 facedown on top of patch 1, matching the edges to be joined. Stitch ¼" from the edge through all three layers.

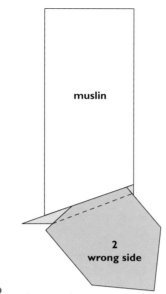

3. Flip patch 2 over and press from the right side. Trim patch 1 as shown.

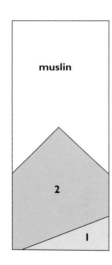

4. Use the same technique to stitch, flip, and press patches 3, 4, 5, and 6, one by one, until the muslin is covered. Use the arrows on the patterns to orient the shapes correctly. Repeat steps 2–4 to make a second crazy-patch panel in mirror image. Work buttonhole stitch in black floss over all the seams.

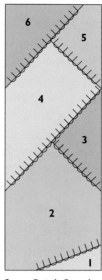

Crazy-Patch Panel
Make 2 (reverse 1)

5. Place a crazy patch panel on each end of the appliquéd mountains panel, right sides together and 6" edges matching. Machine-stitch ¼" from the edge. Press the seam allowances toward the middle panel. Work buttonhole stitch in black floss over the seams. Add the side borders. Press. Add the top and bottom borders. Press.

6. Place the pillow front and back right sides together. Stitch all around, leaving a 5" opening on one edge for turning. Trim the corners diagonally. Turn the pillow right side out. Stuff firmly with fiberfill. Sew the opening closed by hand.

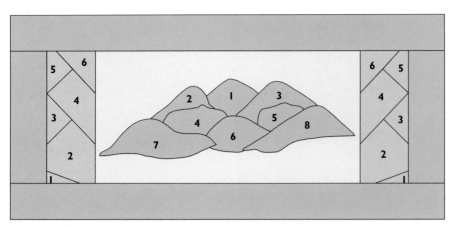

Assembly Diagram

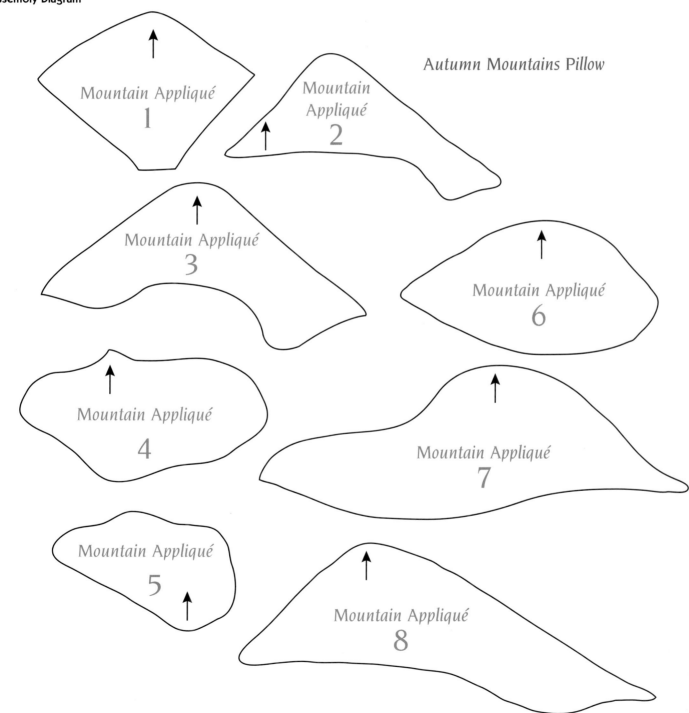

Autumn Mountains Pillow

Mountain Appliqué
1

Mountain Appliqué
2

Mountain Appliqué
3

Mountain Appliqué
6

Mountain Appliqué
4

Mountain Appliqué
7

Mountain Appliqué
5

Mountain Appliqué
8

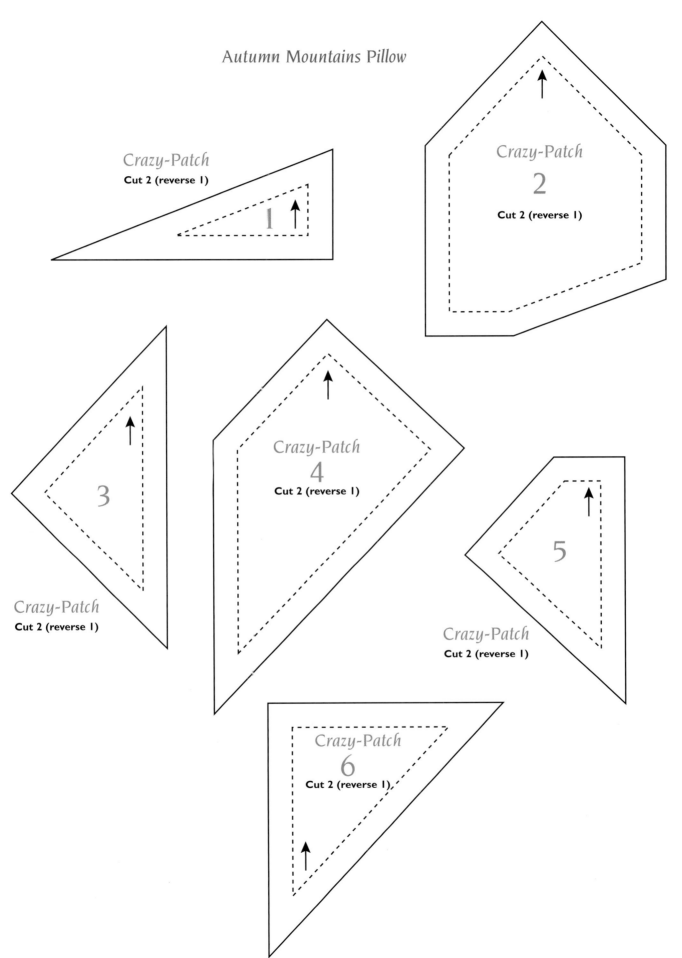

Autumn Mountains Pillow

Crazy-Patch
Cut 2 (reverse 1)
1

Crazy-Patch
2
Cut 2 (reverse 1)

3

Crazy-Patch
Cut 2 (reverse 1)

Crazy-Patch
4
Cut 2 (reverse 1)

5

Crazy-Patch
Cut 2 (reverse 1)

Crazy-Patch
6
Cut 2 (reverse 1)

Squirrel Table Topper

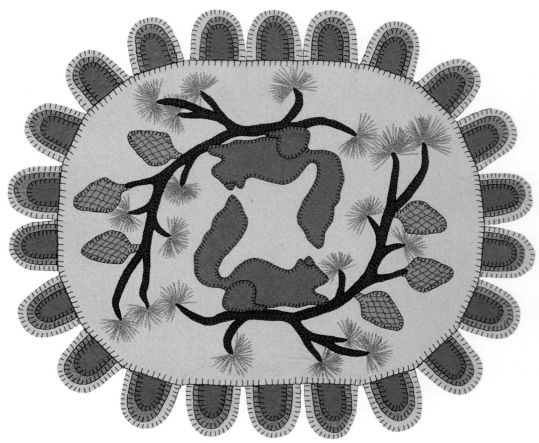

Designed by Barbara Ferguson; 17¹/₂" x 22¹/₂"

Squirrel and pinecone appliqués and a lamb's tongue edging set a perfect mood for autumn meals and buffets. The wool felt pieces are secured to the table topper with buttonhole stitch. Use stem stitch to create the incredibly realistic pine needles.

Materials

Wool felt, 36" wide:
  ³/₄ yard gold for background,
    backing, and lamb's tongues
  Scrap of light rust for appliqués
  ¹/₄ yard dark brown for appliqués
  ¹/₄ yard rust for appliqués and
    lamb's tongues
  ¹/₈ yard olive green for appliqués
    and lamb's tongues

Embroidery floss:
  black (DMC #310)
  medium sage (DMC #3363)
  reddish brown (DMC #975)

BASIC INSTRUCTIONS

Embroidery Design Transfer (page 12)
Buttonhole Stitch (page 11)
Stem Stitch (page 13)

Cutting

Prepare templates A, B, and C, photo-copying at 100%.

From the gold, cut two 18" x 13½" rectangles for the background and backing. Round off the corners, using an 11" to 12" round dinner plate as a template. Also cut 44 lamb's tongues using template A.

Use the patterns on page 96 to prepare nonfusible felt appliqués: 6 light rust pinecones, 2 dark brown branches, 2 rust ears, 2 rust squirrels, and 2 rust hind legs.

From the olive green, cut 22 lamb's tongues using template B.

From the rust, cut 22 lamb's tongues using template C.

Assembly

1. Lay the large gold background piece right side up. Arrange the pinecone, branch, and squirrel appliqués on top, as shown in the project photograph (page 94). Pin the pinecone appliqués in place. Remove the other pieces.

2. Using reddish brown floss and long straight stitches, work a cross-hatch design on each pinecone through both layers. Pin the branch appliqués back in position. Using black floss, work buttonhole stitch around the branch and pinecone edges, securing them in place.

3. Using medium sage floss, embroider pine needles in stem stitch at the tip of each branch. Refer to the project photograph (page 94).

4. Position the squirrel ear, body, and hind leg appliqués on the piece. Work buttonhole stitch in black floss around the edges.

5. Place an olive green B on a gold A, straight edges matching. Work buttonhole stitch in black floss around the curved edge of B through both layers. Layer and stitch a rust C to B in the same way, sewing through all three layers. Back the unit with a second gold A. Work buttonhole stitch around the outside curved edge to join the layers together. Repeat to make 22 layered lamb's tongues.

6. Arrange the lamb's tongues around the appliquéd piece, right sides up, straight edges matching, and evenly spaced all around. Slip each tongue ¼" under the outside edge and pin. Slip the gold backing underneath, match the edges, and pin. Work buttonhole stitch in black floss around the outside edge through all layers, securing the tongues and removing the pins as you go.

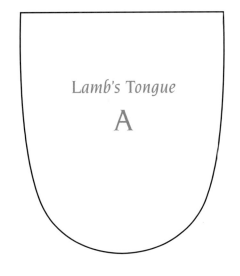

Lamb's Tongue

A

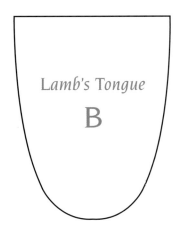

Lamb's Tongue

B

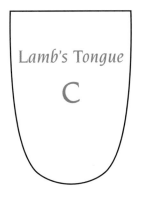

Lamb's Tongue

C

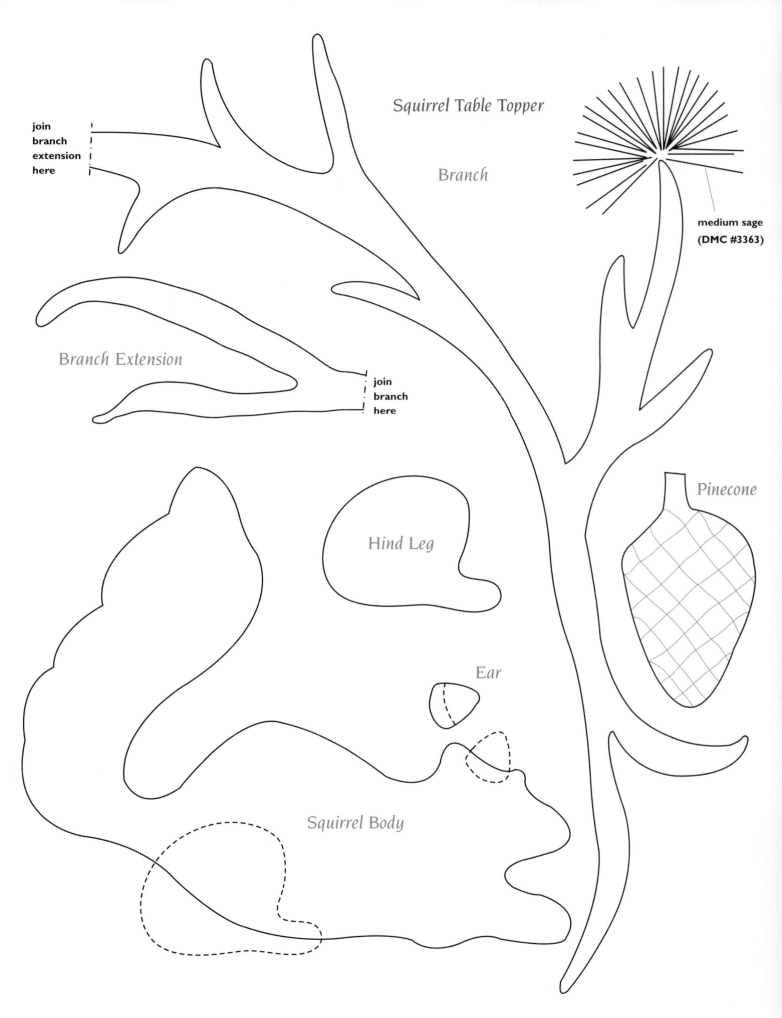

Squirrel Table Topper

Branch

join
branch
extension
here

medium sage
(DMC #3363)

Branch Extension

join
branch
here

Pinecone

Hind Leg

Ear

Squirrel Body

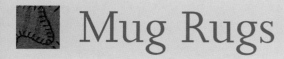 # Mug Rugs

Designed by Jean Wells and Lawry Thorn; 4" diameter and 4" square

W ool felt coasters, dubbed "mug rugs," are just the thing to slide under a cup of coffee or hot chocolate. This is the perfect project for children who want to surprise relatives and teachers with holiday gifts they've made themselves. Each coaster works up quickly, for those occasions when you need a small gift in a hurry.

Materials

For One Mug Rug

Scraps of wool felt:
  black for base
  rust or olive for appliqué background
Scrap of contrasting plaid flannel for
  appliqué
Paper-backed fusible web
Black embroidery floss (DMC #310)

BASIC INSTRUCTIONS

Buttonhole Stitch (page 11)
French Knot (page 13)

Cutting

For a round rug mug, prepare circle templates A and B, photocopying at 100%.

From the black wool felt, cut either one 4" x 4" square or one circle A for the base.

From the rust or olive wool felt, cut either one 3½" x 3½" square or one circle B for the appliqué background.

Use the bird pattern, the bear cub pattern on page 77, or another small pattern to prepare a fusible appliqué from the plaid flannel.

Assembly

1. Center the appliqué on the background piece. Fuse in place.

2. Work buttonhole stitch in black floss around the edge of the appliqué. For the bird, work three straight stitches for each foot and a French knot for the eye.

3. Center the appliquéd square or circle on the black base. Work buttonhole stitch around the inner edge to join the pieces together.

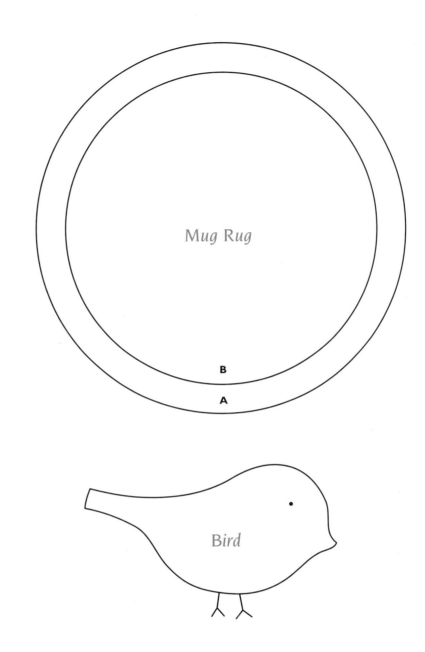

Mug Rug

B

A

Bird

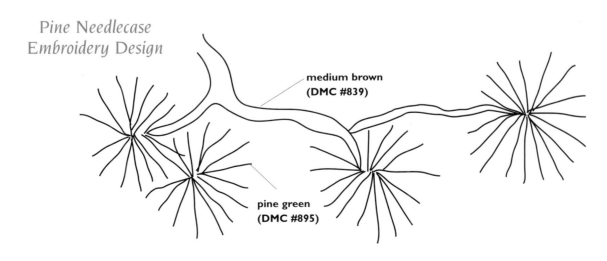

Pine Needlecase Embroidery Design

medium brown
(DMC #839)

pine green
(DMC #895)

Pine Needlecase

Designed by Jean Wells and Lawry Thorn; 8" x 12" opened, 8" x 4¹/₂" closed

W hat quilter or stitcher doesn't need a place to keep needles, a thimble, and small scissors handy? Make this wallet-style needlecase from washable wool felt and flannel.

Materials

Light gold flannel, at least 4" x 8", for embroidery

Wool felt:

14" x 20" brown for body

4" x 12" rust for pocket and needle book

4" x 12" olive for needle book

Embroidery floss:

rust (DMC #919)

medium brown (DMC #839)

pine green (DMC #895)

olive green (DMC #935)

BASIC INSTRUCTIONS

Buttonhole Stitch (page 11)

Embroidery Design Transfer (12)

Stem Stitch (page 13)

Cutting

From the brown wool felt, cut two 8" x 12" rectangles.

From the rust wool felt, cut one 3" x 6" rectangle for the pocket and one 2½" x 5" rectangle for the needle book.

From the olive green wool felt, cut one 2½" x 6½" rectangle and one 2½" x 4" rectangle, both for the needle book.

Assembly

1. Transfer the pine bough pattern (page 98) to the light gold flannel. Embroider the design in stem stitch, using medium brown floss for the branch and pine green floss for the pine needles. Trim the panel to 4" x 8". Fold and press the long edges ½" to the wrong side. Fold and press the short edges ½" to the wrong side.

2. Lay one brown wool felt rectangle right side up. Position the embroidered panel ½" in from the lower and side edges. Pin in place. Using rust floss, work buttonhole stitch around the edge of the panel to secure it to the wool felt. Set aside.

Front

3. Stack and center the three needle book rectangles in size order. Using rust floss, sew a running stitch down the "spine" through all three layers as shown.

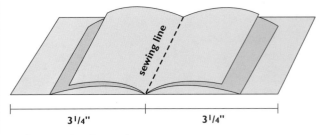

Making the Needle Book

3¼"   3¼"

4. Lay the other brown wool felt rectangle right side up. Position the needlebook ¾" in from the lower and side edges. To secure it in place, work buttonhole stitch in rust floss around the edges of the larger olive green rectangle only, so that the "pages" turn freely.

5. Center the pocket on the same brown wool felt piece, 4½" from the top and bottom edges. Make two small tucks in the lower edge of the pocket, drawing it in to measure 4" across. Pin the bottom and side edges, letting the sides flare out slightly. Work buttonhole stitch in olive green floss to secure the pinned edges.

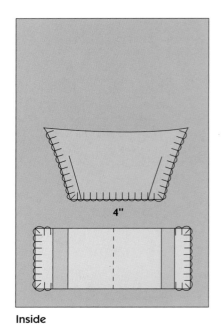

4"

Inside

6. To complete the needlecase, lay the front piece facedown with the embroidered panel at the top. Lay the inside piece on top, right side up, with the needle book at the bottom. Work buttonhole stitch in rust floss around the edges to join the pieces together. Fold the completed needlecase into thirds so that the pine embroidery falls on the front cover.

Designed by Jean Wells and Lawry Thorn; 7³/₄" x 10"

Tuck a small gift into this wool felt stocking as an alternative to gift wrap. The lucky recipient will have two gifts in one—the contents plus a pretty stocking to hang in the kitchen or family room to hold shopping coupons, lunch money, or a bunch of dried flowers.

Materials

Wool felt, 36" wide:
  ¹/₂ yard dark green for stocking
  Scraps of olive green, beige, and rust for mock cuff, tree appliqués, and hanging loop
Scrap of flannel in a coordinating plaid for bear appliqué
Black embroidery floss (DMC #310)

BASIC INSTRUCTIONS

Buttonhole Stitch Appliqué (page 10)

Cutting

Use the stocking pattern (page 125) and mock cuff pattern (below), photocopying at 100%.

From the dark green, cut two stockings and one $\frac{3}{8}$" x 4" strip for a hanging loop.

From the olive green, cut one mock cuff.

Use the reverse of the pine tree and bear cub patterns on page 77 to prepare 3 fusible appliqués: 1 beige tree, 1 rust tree, and 1 rust plaid bear cub.

Assembly

1. Lay one stocking right side up. Place the mock cuff at the top and pin in place. Arrange the three appliqués underneath, overlapping them as shown in the project photograph (page 101). Fuse the appliqués in place, working from background to foreground.

2. Work buttonhole stitch in black floss around the edges of the cuff and each appliqué.

3. Place the two stocking pieces wrong sides together. Work buttonhole stitch around the outside curved edge to join the pieces together. Leave the top straight edge open.

4. Fold the $\frac{3}{8}$" x 4" strip in half. Tack the ends to the top right corner of the stocking for a hanging loop.

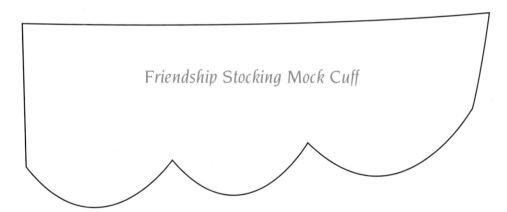

Friendship Stocking Mock Cuff

For stocking pattern, see page 125

WINTER

Piney Woods Quilt

Designed by Jean Wells and Lawry Thorn; 54¼" x 65½"

Embroidered chickadees perched on pine boughs enhance the wintry feeling of this quilt. All the blocks use a creamy white background, suggesting a blanket of new-fallen snow. If you'd like a forest that appears even more dense, substitute Pine Trees for the Double Four-Patch blocks.

Materials

Flannel fabrics:

3 yards creamy white for embroidery, Pine Tree blocks, Double Four-Patch blocks, and border

¼ yard each of five or six different greens for Pine Tree blocks

¼ yard light brown for Pine Tree Blocks

¼ yard gold for Double Four-Patch blocks

⅞ yard red plaid for Double Four-Patch blocks and border squares

¾ yard light tan plaid for setting triangles

⅜ yard for binding

3½ yards backing

59" x 70" batting

Embroidery floss:

pine green (DMC #895)

dark brown (DMC #3031)

dark sage (DMC #3362)

medium gray (DMC #647)

dark gray (DMC #535)

Template plastic (for template HDH)

BASIC INSTRUCTIONS

Embroidery Design Transfer (page 12)

Stem Stitch (page 13)

Double Four-Patch (page 15)

Pine Tree (page 22)

Finishing a Quilt (page 23)

Cutting

EMBROIDERED BLOCKS

From the creamy white, cut two 8½" x 42" strips; cut into five 8½" squares for the chickadee blocks. Cut two 4¾" x 42" strips; cut into two 4¾" x 11¾" rectangles and four 4¾" x 9⅝" rectangles for pine bough units.

PINE TREE BLOCKS

Prepare templates B, C, F, G, and HDH (pages 88–89 and 108), photocopying at 100%. Use template plastic for HDH.

From the various greens, cut a total of eight 3⅞" squares; cut in half diagonally for 16 half-square triangles (A). Use the templates to cut 16 B and 16 C to match the A's.

From the light brown, cut two 1½" x 42" strips (D). Cut one 1⅞" x 42" strip; cut into eight 1⅞" squares; cut each square in half diagonally for 16 half-square triangles (E).

From the creamy white, cut 32 pieces each (reverse 16) using templates F and G. Cut four 4" x 42" strips (H).

DOUBLE FOUR-PATCH BLOCKS

From the creamy white and the gold, cut three 2½" x 42" strips each.

From the red plaid, cut three 4½" x 42" strips; cut into twenty 4½" squares.

LARGE SETTING TRIANGLES

From the light tan plaid, cut two 12⅝" x 42" strips. Cut into five 12⅝" squares; cut diagonally in both directions for 20 quarter-square setting triangles (discard 2).

BORDER

From the red plaid, cut four 3½" x 42" strips; cut into thirty-eight 3½" squares (I).

From the creamy white, cut two 5½" x 42" strips; cut into fourteen 5½" squares; cut diagonally in both directions for 56 quarter-square setting triangles (J). Cut two 3" x 42" strips; cut into twenty 3" squares; cut in half diagonally for 40 half-square setting triangles (K).

Assembly

1. Place the five 8½" creamy white background squares on point. Transfer the chickadee pattern (page 109) to each square, reversing the design for two of them. Transfer the pine bough pattern (page 108) to the six white border rectangles. Embroider each design in stem stitch, using the floss colors indicated on the patterns.

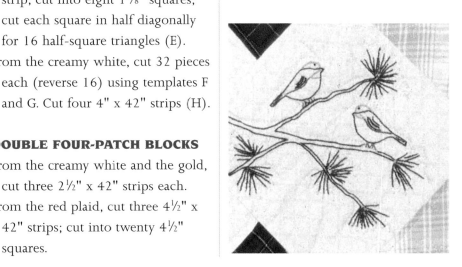

2. Stitch the Pine Tree pieces together to make 16 FBF and 16 GCG units. Stitch a white H strip to each side of the light brown D strips. Press toward the darker fabric. Align the plastic template for piece HDH on top to mark and cut 16 units.

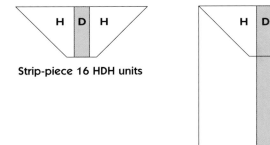

Strip-piece 16 HDH units

3. Join the pieced units from step 2 and triangles A and E to make 16 Pine Tree blocks.

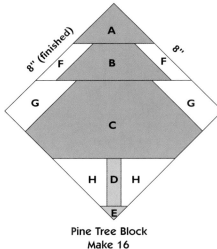

Pine Tree Block
Make 16

4. Stitch the creamy white and gold 2½" x 42" strips together in pairs. Press. Cut into forty 2½" segments. Stitch the segments together in pairs to make 20 white-and-gold Four-Patch units. Join each unit to a 4½" red plaid square, making 20 identical units. Join the units together in pairs for 10 Double Four-Patch blocks.

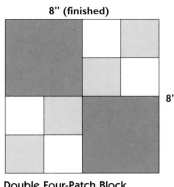

8" (finished)

Double Four-Patch Block
Make 10

5. Lay out the embroidered and pieced blocks on point, referring to the quilt photograph (page 104) and quilt diagram for placement. Fill in the edges with the light tan plaid setting triangles. Stitch the blocks and setting triangles together in diagonal rows. Stitch the remaining setting triangles together in pairs for the corners. Press. Join the rows together, pressing after each addition. Add the corners last. Press.

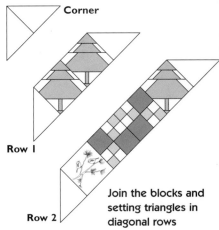

Join the blocks and setting triangles in diagonal rows

6. To begin the border, stitch 2 white J triangles to opposite edges of a red square I. Press. Make 18 units. Stitch a white J triangle to each remaining red square I, for 20 units. Press.

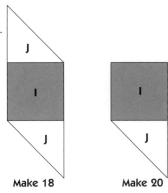

Make 18   **Make 20**

7. Arrange 3 JIJ and 2 IJ units in diagonal rows. Stitch the rows together. Press. Add a white K triangle to each corner. Press. Make six 5-square units. Join the remaining IJ units together in pairs and add corner triangles to make four 2-square units.

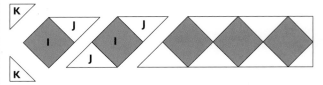

5-Square Unit
Make 6

2-Square Unit
Make 4

8. For each side border, join two $4^{3}/_{4}$" x $9^{5}/_{8}$" embroidered rectangles, two 2-square units, and one 5-square unit, as shown. Press. For the top and bottom borders, join one $4^{3}/_{4}$" x $11^{3}/_{4}$" embroidered rectangle and two 5-square units. Press. Add the side borders to the quilt. Press. Add the top and bottom borders to the quilt. Press.

9. Layer and finish the quilt. *Piney Woods* features diagonal machine quilting through the small Four-Patch blocks. The larger squares are stitched $^{1}/_{4}$" from the outer edge, and in the creamy white squares, the stitching lines form gentle arcs that end at the corners. The embroidered pine bough and chickadee designs are outline-quilted, and each patchwork tree contains a free-form tree shape within it.

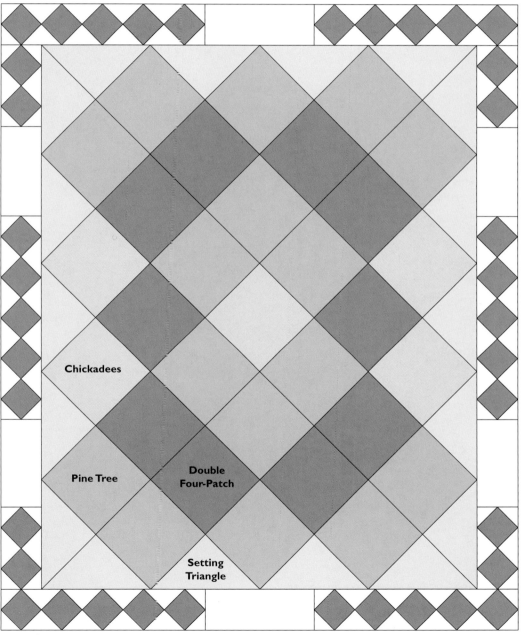

Quilt Diagram

Piney Woods Quilt

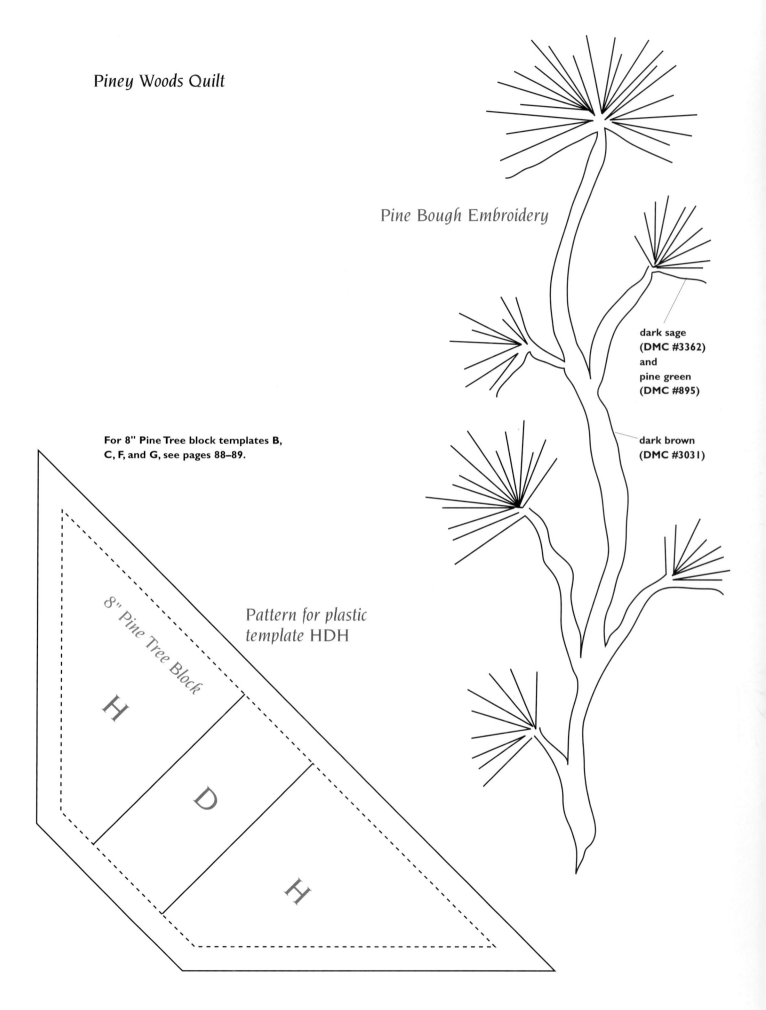

Pine Bough Embroidery

dark sage
(DMC #3362)
and
pine green
(DMC #895)

dark brown
(DMC #3031)

For 8" Pine Tree block templates B, C, F, and G, see pages 88–89.

Pattern for plastic template HDH

8" Pine Tree Block

H

D

H

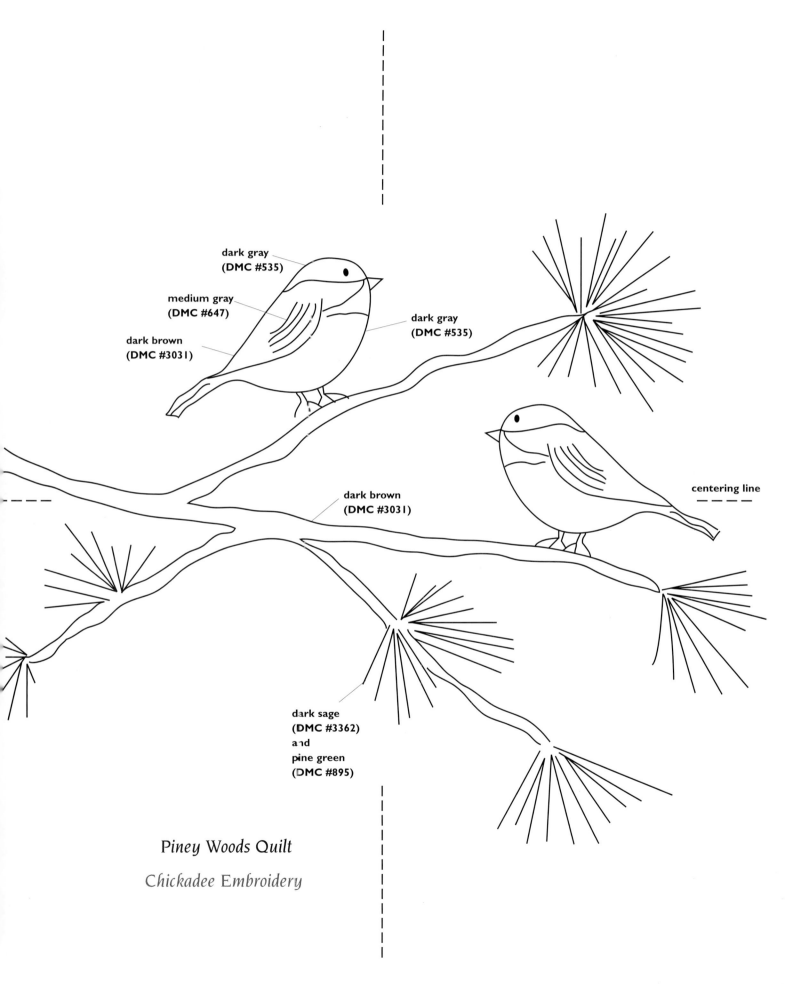

dark gray
(DMC #535)

medium gray
(DMC #647)

dark brown
(DMC #3031)

dark gray
(DMC #535)

dark brown
(DMC #3031)

centering line

dark sage
(DMC #3362)
and
pine green
(DMC #895)

Piney Woods Quilt

Chickadee Embroidery

Starry Night Quilt

Designed by Jean Wells and Lawry Thorn; 64$\frac{1}{2}$" x 64$\frac{1}{2}$"

What could be better for the long, dark nights of winter than hot cocoa, a rocker, and a quilt to snuggle in? *Starry Night* features deep red stars that twinkle at the points and radiate a golden glow—a reminder of evenings when the sky is clear, the stars are bright, and temperatures are well below the comfort zone.

Materials

Flannel fabrics:

- ¼ yard each light red and red-and-white plaid for Pine Star blocks
- ⅜ yard each medium red and dark red for Pine Star blocks
- 3 yards black print for Pine Star blocks, Nine-Patch blocks, sashing, and border
- ⅞ yard tobacco brown print for Nine-Patch blocks
- 4 yards backing
- ⅜ yard for binding
- 69" x 69" batting

BASIC INSTRUCTIONS

Nine-Patch (page 15)

Pine Star (page 21)

Finishing a Quilt (page 23)

Cutting

PINE STAR BLOCKS, HALF-BLOCKS, AND QUARTER-BLOCKS

Prepare templates A, D, and G (page 113), photocopying at 100%.

From the light red, cut 32 squares using template A.

From the red-and-white plaid, cut one 4¼" strip; cut into eight 4¼" squares; cut each square diagonally in both directions for 32 quarter-square triangles (B).

From the medium red, cut two 4¼" squares; cut each square diagonally in both directions for 8 quarter-square triangles (B) (discard 2). Use the templates to cut 10 D and 6 G.

From the dark red, cut one 4¼" square; cut diagonally in both directions for 4 quarter-square triangles (B) (discard 2). Use the templates to cut 14 D and 2 G.

From the black print, cut two 7¼" x 42" strips; cut into six 7¼" squares; cut each square diagonally in both directions for 24 quarter-square triangles (C). Cut three 3½" x 42" strips; cut into thirty-two 3½" squares (E). Cut one 3⅞" x 42" strip; cut into eight 3⅞" squares; cut each square in half diagonally for 16 half-square triangles (F).

NINE-PATCH BLOCKS AND HALF-BLOCKS

From the black print, cut four 4½" x 42" strips.

From the tobacco brown print, cut five 4½" x 42" strips.

SASHING

From the black print, cut twelve 2½" x 42" strips; cut into twenty-four 2½" x 12½" strips and sixteen 2½" x 6½" strips.

From the tobacco brown print, cut one 2½" x 42" strip; cut into sixteen 2½" squares.

BORDER

From the black print, cut six 4½" x 42" strips. Piece together end to end, and cut into two 4½" x 56½"

side border strips and two 4½" x 64½" top and bottom border strips.

Assembly

1. Make 5 Pine Star blocks, using 2 dark red D pieces and 2 medium red D pieces in each block.

12" (finished)

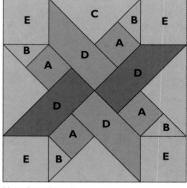

Pine Star Block
Make 5

2. For the Pine Star half-blocks and quarter-blocks, make four more ABCDE units, using up the remaining dark red D's. Remember to use the Y-seam construction when adding piece E.

3. Stitch an F triangle to each G parallelogram. Press.

Make 6   Make 2

4. Stitch two different B triangles to opposite edges of each remaining A square, forming a parallelogram. Press. Sew an E square and an F triangle to each BAB unit.

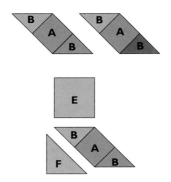

5. Complete the Y-seam construction to join the units from steps 2, 3, and 4. Repeat to make 4 identical Pine Star half-blocks.

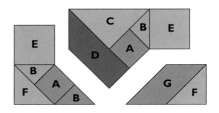

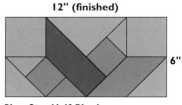

Pine Star Half-Block
Make 4

6. Stitch the remaining eight units together to make 4 Pine Star quarter-blocks for the quilt corners. Set all the completed Pine Star blocks and units aside.

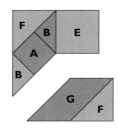

6" (finished)

Make 2   Make 2

Pine Star Quarter-Blocks

7. For the Nine-Patch blocks and half-blocks, stitch the 4½"-wide tobacco brown and black print strips together in groups of three, using a ¼" seam allowance. Make two sets with a black print strip in the middle and one set with a tobacco brown strip in the middle. Press toward the darker fabric. Cut the two matching sets into a total of sixteen 4½" segments. Cut the remaining set into four 4½" segments and eight 2½" segments.

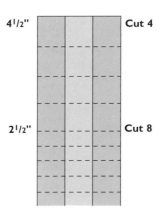

4½"   Cut 16

4½"   Cut 4

2½"   Cut 8

8. Arrange the segments in rows and join together to make 4 Nine-Patch blocks and 8 Nine-Patch half-blocks.

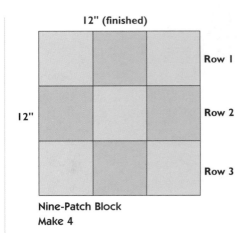

12" (finished)

12"   Row 1

Row 2

Row 3

Nine-Patch Block
Make 4

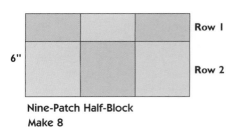

6"   Row 1

Row 2

Nine-Patch Half-Block
Make 8

9. Lay out the nine full-size Pine Star and Nine-Patch blocks, referring to the quilt diagram for placement. Add the half-blocks and quarter blocks around the edges. Join the blocks in each row together with 4 sashing strips; use the shorter sashing strips for rows 1 and 5. Stitch the remaining sashing strips and squares together to make 4 horizontal sashing strips, and join the quilt rows together. Add the side borders. Press. Add the top and bottom borders. Press.

10. Layer and finish the quilt. *Starry Night* features diagonal machine quilting through many of the squares and rectangles. The stars are quilted ¼" from the outer edge in variegated thread, while the inner points are filled with a swirly design. Loose (not close) swirls and gentle curves fill in behind the Pine Star blocks.

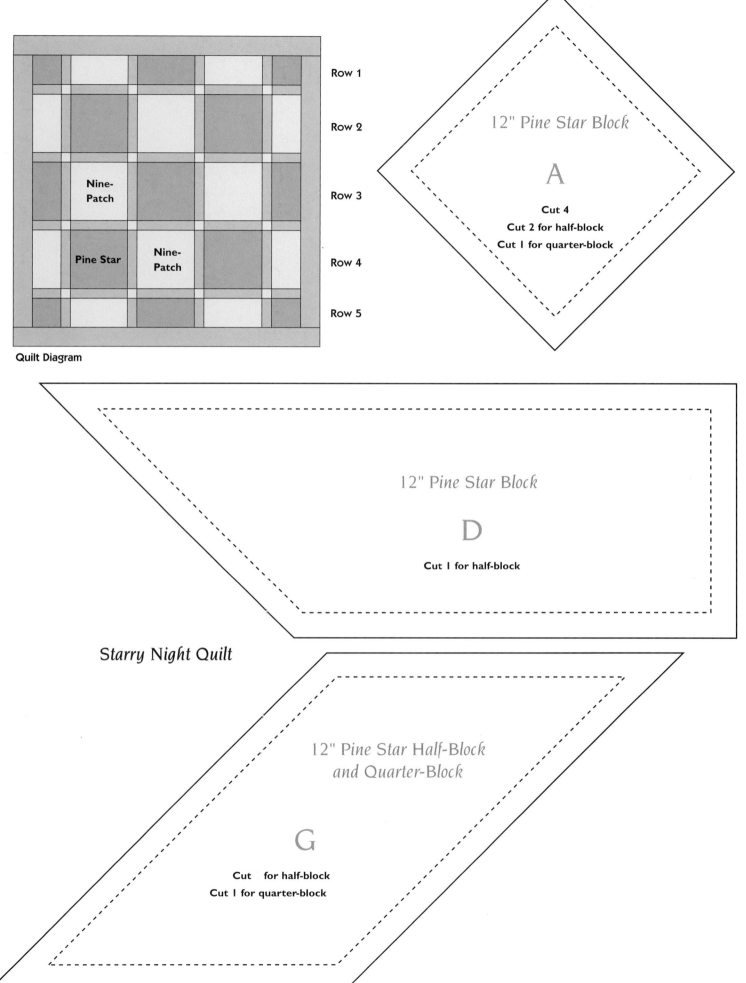

Row 1

Row 2

Row 3

Row 4

Row 5

Nine-Patch

Pine Star

Nine-Patch

Quilt Diagram

12" Pine Star Block

A

Cut 4
Cut 2 for half-block
Cut 1 for quarter-block

12" Pine Star Block

D

Cut 1 for half-block

Starry Night Quilt

12" Pine Star Half-Block
and Quarter-Block

G

Cut   for half-block
Cut 1 for quarter-block

Checkerboard Pine Quilt

Designed by Jean Wells and Lawry Thorn; 22$\frac{1}{2}$" x 22$\frac{1}{2}$"

Coarsely woven off-white linen squares step in for flannel in this embroidered pine bough quilt. Orient the embroidered squares as shown for a wall hanging, or turn the blocks so the pinecones are in the four outer corners if the quilt will be placed on a tabletop and viewed from all directions. The color palette carries this quilt from winter through early spring, when the moonlight changes from off-white to soft yellow.

Materials

3/8 yard off-white medium-weight linen for embroidery

Flannel fabrics:

1 yard yellow plaid for sashing/ border, backing, and binding

1/4 yard black for sashing/border

27" x 27" batting

Embroidery floss:

dark brown (DMC #3031)

reddish brown (DMC #975)

pine green (DMC #895)

BASIC INSTRUCTIONS

Embroidery Design Transfer (page 12)

Stem Stitch (page 13)

Checkerboard Strips (page 14)

Finishing a Quilt (page 23)

Cutting

From the linen, cut four 9" squares. Serge or zigzag the outer edges to prevent raveling. The squares will be trimmed to 8½" after the embroidery is completed.

From each flannel, cut five 1½" x 42" strips for the checkerboard sashing and border. Set aside the remaining yellow plaid flannel for the backing and binding.

Assembly

1. Transfer the pine bough pattern (page 116) to each 9" off-white linen square, reversing the design on two squares. Embroider each design in stem stitch, using the floss colors indicated on the pattern. When the embroidery is completed, trim each square to 8½".

2. Stitch the yellow plaid and black flannel strips together in pairs. Press toward the darker strip. Cut each double strip into 1½" segments until you have 114 segments.

3. Join the segments together, alternating the colors, to make six 2x8 checkerboard strips for the horizontal sashing/borders and three 2x22 checkerboard strips for the vertical sashing/borders.

4. Arrange the embroidered blocks and checkerboard strips as shown in the quilt diagram; orient the pine bough embroidery as shown in the quilt photograph (page 114) or as desired. Join the blocks and horizontal sashing/border strips into two columns. Press. Join the columns and the vertical sashing/border strips. Press.

5. Layer and finish the quilt. *Checkerboard Pine* uses in-the-ditch quilting to define the blocks. Echo quilting calls attention to the embroidered pine boughs.

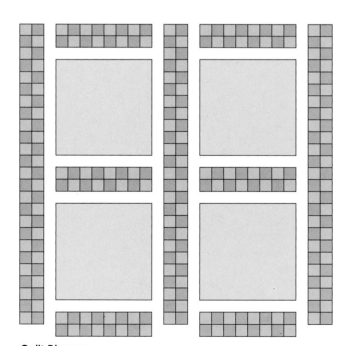

Quilt Diagram

Checkerboard Pine Quilt

Pine Bough Embroidery

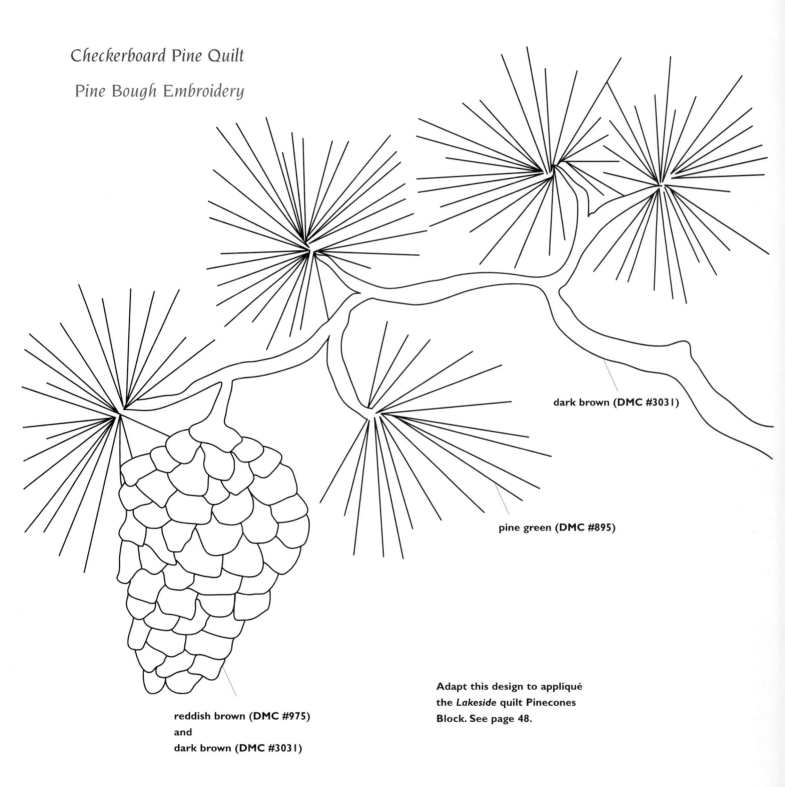

dark brown (DMC #3031)

pine green (DMC #895)

reddish brown (DMC #975)
and
dark brown (DMC #3031)

**Adapt this design to appliqué
the *Lakeside* quilt Pinecones
Block. See page 48.**

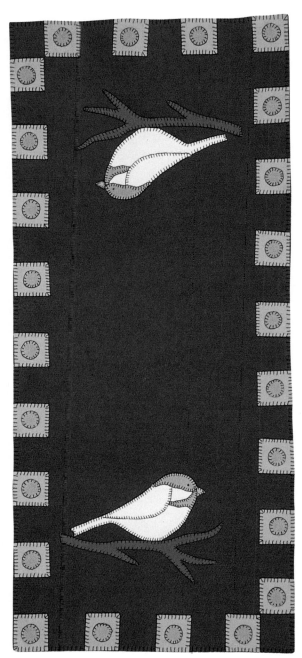

Designed by Jean Wells and Lawry Thorn; 16" x 36"

Chickadees perch at each end of this wool felt table topper, leaving space in the middle for a bowl of pinecones or a holiday wreath and candle.

Materials

Wool felt, 36" wide:
  1 yard deep olive for background and backing
  ⅛ yard gray for appliqués
  ⅛ yard gold for appliqués
  ⅛ yard off-white for appliqués
  ⅛ yard brown for appliqués
Black embroidery floss (DMC #310)

BASIC INSTRUCTIONS

Buttonhole Stitch (page 11)

Cutting

From the deep olive, cut two 16" x 36" rectangles for the background and backing.

From the gray, cut twenty-four 1" circles (we traced around a quarter). From the gold, cut twenty-four 2" squares.

Use the patterns below and on page 119 to cut nonfusible appliqués: 2 off-white chickadee bodies, 2 off-white wings, 2 gray crests, 2 gray throats, 2 gold beaks, and 2 brown branches.

Assembly

1. Center a gray circle on each gold square. Work buttonhole stitch in black floss around each circle.

2. Lay the background rectangle right side up. Arrange the gold squares around the edges, evenly spaced, as shown in project photograph (page 117). Pin in place. Work buttonhole stitch in black floss on the three inside edges of each gold square. Leave the outer edges unstitched.

3. Arrange the chickadee and branch appliqués at each end of the table topper. Work buttonhole stitch around the edges of each branch. For each chickadee, embroider the inside edges of the throat, wing, and crest first, and then stitch around the outer edge. Add the beak last. Work a French knot for the eye.

QUILTER'S TIP

To hold nonfusible appliqués in place temporarily, use a fabric glue stick.

4. Layer the table topper and backing wrong sides together. Pin. Work buttonhole stitch in black floss around the outside edge, anchoring the border squares as you go.

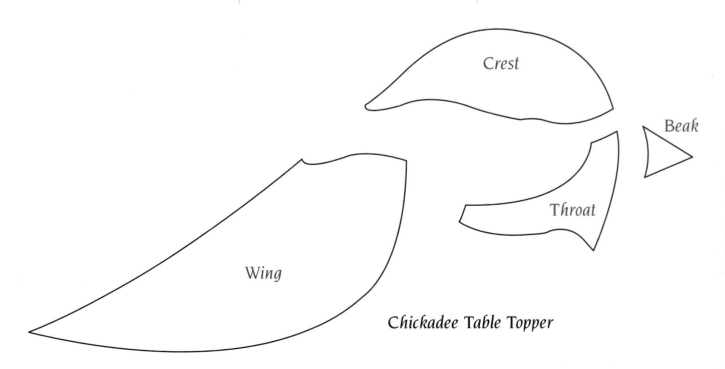

Chickadee Table Topper

Chickadee Table Topper

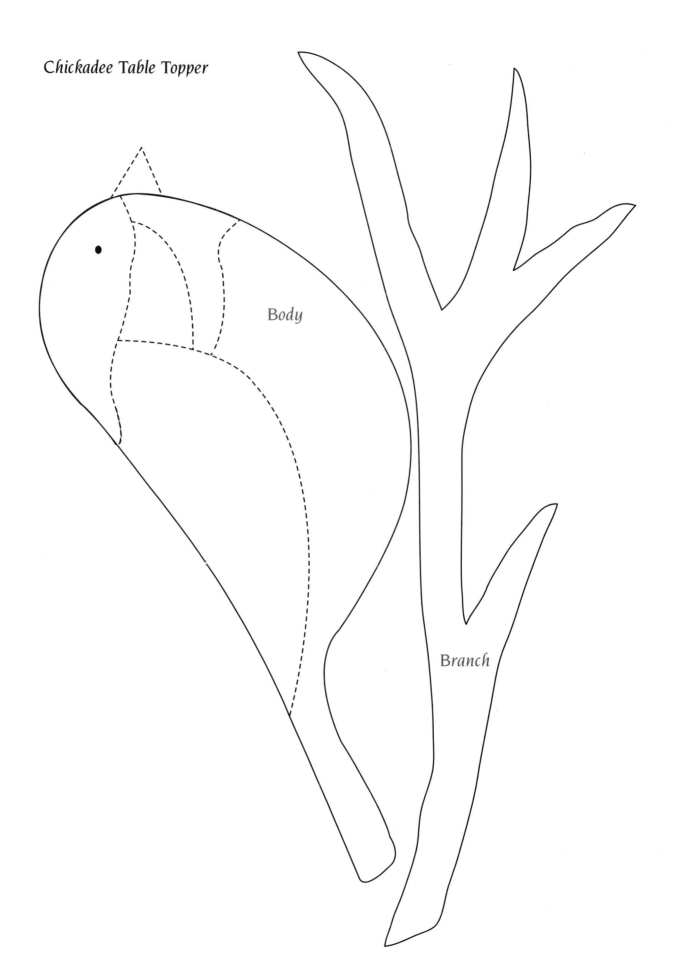

Body

Branch

Chickadee Tree Skirt

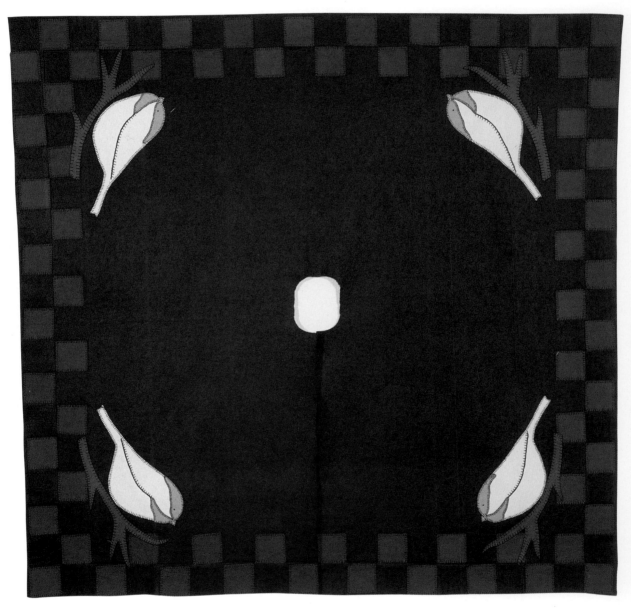

Designed by Jean Wells and Lawry Thorn; 42" x 42"

A wool felt square sets the stage for a tree skirt with an appliquéd checkerboard border. The grid design is softened by chickadees perching in the four corners. All the appliqués are edged in black buttonhole stitch.

Materials

Wool felt, 36" wide unless noted:
  1¼ yards dark green for background (72" wide)
  ¼ yard cranberry red for squares
  ¼ yard off-white for appliqués
  ¼ yard brown for appliqués
  6" x 8" gray for appliqués
  Scrap of gold for appliqués
Black embroidery floss (DMC #310)

BASIC INSTRUCTIONS

Buttonhole Stitch (page 11)
Stem Stitch (page 13)
French Knot (page 13)

Cutting

From the dark green, cut a 42" square.

From the cranberry red, cut seventy-two 2" squares.

Use the patterns on page 122 to cut the nonfusible appliqués: 4 off-white chickadee bodies, 4 gray crests, 4 gray throats, 4 gold beaks, and 4 brown branches.

Assembly

1. Lay the 42" dark green background square wrong side up. Measure to find the center of the square and make a small mark, as shown in the diagram. Also mark the midpoint of one edge. Draw a line connecting these two points. Draw a 4"-diameter circle around the center mark (we used a clear glass saucer as a template). Starting on the outside edge, cut on the marked line for 5" only. The cut will be completed later, to avoid putting stress on the felt as it is appliquéd.

2. Lay the background square right side up. Arrange the 2" cranberry squares in a double row, checkerboard-style, around the edges. Allow a sliver of dark green wool felt to show around the outer edge, and don't let the squares touch one another at the corners. The pieces are sized to allow for this breathing room. For a quirky look, omit a few squares and offset the checkerboard grid, as shown in the project photograph (page 120). Work buttonhole stitch in black floss around each small square.

3. Arrange the chickadee and branch appliqués in each corner, layering the pieces as indicated on the pattern. Work buttonhole stitch in black floss around the edges of each branch. For each chickadee, work the wing line first in stem stitch and then in buttonhole stitch. Work buttonhole stitch on the inside edges of the throat and crest, and then stitch around the entire outer edge. Add the beak last. Work a French knot for the eye.

4. Finish cutting the slit and the round opening at the center.

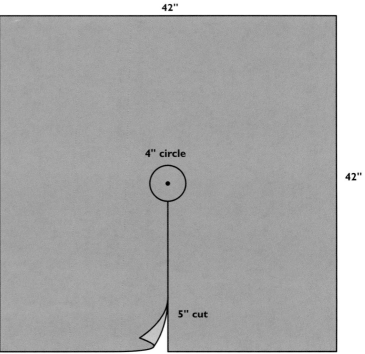

42"

4" circle

42"

5" cut

Cutting Diagram

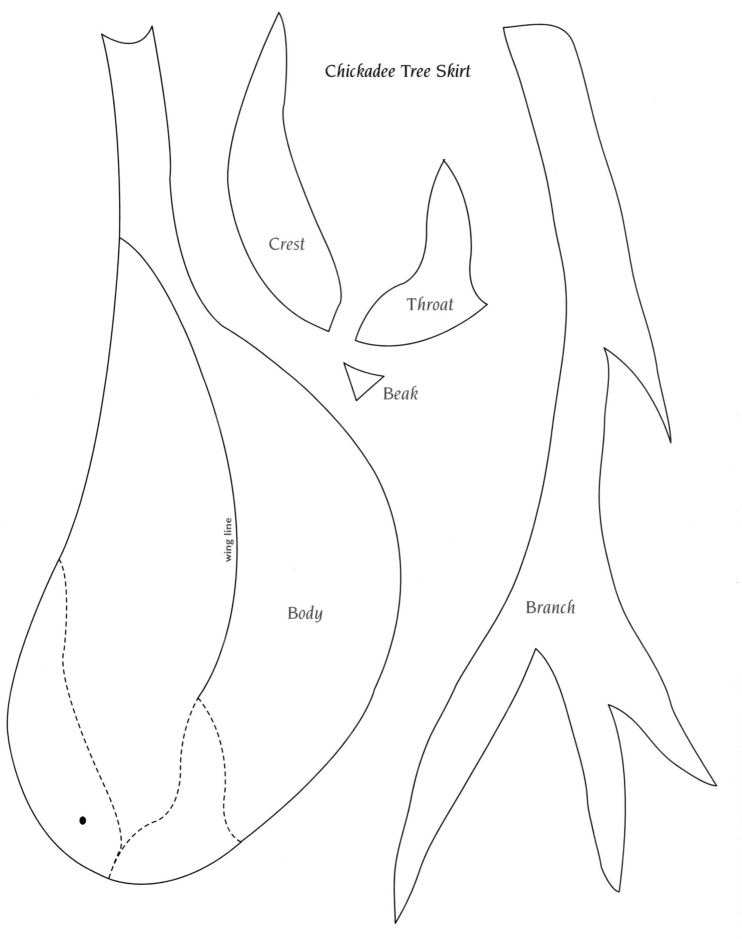

Chickadee Tree Skirt

Crest

Throat

Beak

wing line

Body

Branch

Holiday Stockings

Designed by Jean Wells and Lawry Thorn;
large stocking, 7³/₄" x 10";
small stockings, each 4³/₄" x 6"

Here's a holiday version of the friendship stocking featured on page 101. Use our chickadee appliqué or select another motif as a decorative accent. Reduce the pattern to make tree ornaments or gift package tie-ons.

Materials

For 10" Stocking
Wool felt:

 12" x 18" yard cranberry red for stocking

 4" x 6" dark green for mock cuff scraps of white, brown, and gold for appliqués

Paper-backed fusible web

Black embroidery floss (DMC #310)

For 6" Stocking
Wool felt:

 8" x 12" piece for stocking scraps for mock cuff and hanging loop

Black embroidery floss (DMC #310)

BASIC INSTRUCTIONS

Buttonhole Stitch Appliqué (page 10)

French Knot (page 13)

Cutting

10" STOCKING

Use the stocking and cuff patterns (page 125 and below), photocopying at 100%.

From the cranberry red, cut 2 stockings.

From the dark green, cut 1 mock cuff and one $\frac{3}{8}$" x 4" strip for a hanging loop.

Use the chickadee pattern on page 125 to prepare the fusible appliqués: 1 white chickadee, 1 yellow beak, and 1 brown branch.

6" STOCKING

Use the stocking and cuff patterns (page 125 and below), photocopying at 60%.

From the assorted felts, cut 2 stockings, 1 cuff, and one $\frac{3}{8}$" x 4" strip for the hanging loop.

Assembly

10" STOCKING

1. Lay the mock cuff right side up. Arrange the chickadee appliqués on the cuff, as shown in the photograph (page 123). Fuse in place. Work buttonhole stitch in black floss around the edges of each appliqué. Work a French knot for the eye.

2. Pin the cuff, right side up, to one stocking. Work buttonhole stitch across the top edge and lower scalloped edge only.

3. Place both stockings wrong sides together. Work buttonhole stitch around the outside curved edge to join the pieces together. Leave the top straight edge open.

4. Fold the $\frac{3}{8}$" x 4" strip in half. Tack the ends to the top right corner of the stocking for a hanging loop.

6" STOCKING

Follow the assembly instructions for the 10" stocking, steps 2–4, to make this smaller version.

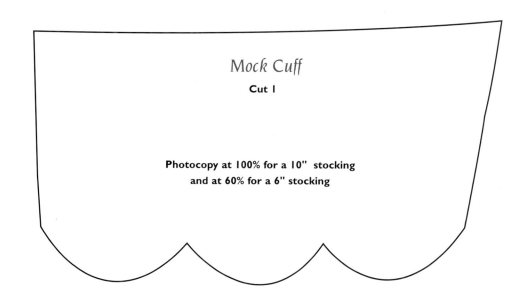

Mock Cuff

Cut 1

Photocopy at 100% for a 10" stocking and at 60% for a 6" stocking

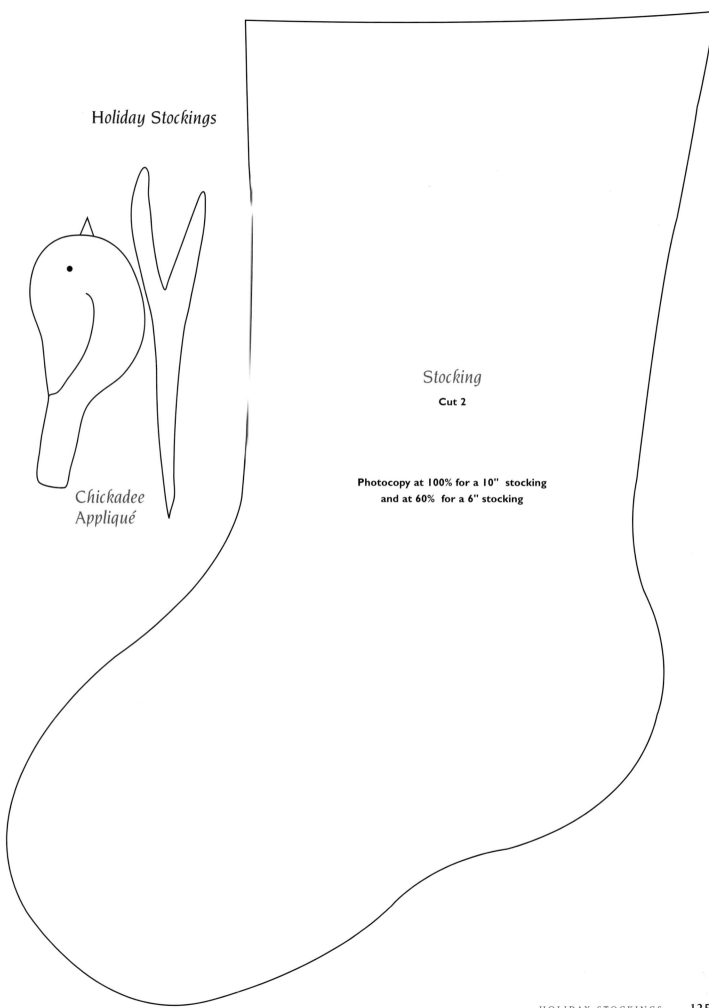

Holiday Stockings

Chickadee
Appliqué

Stocking

Cut 2

**Photocopy at 100% for a 10" stocking
and at 60% for a 6" stocking**

Meet the Authors

Lawry Thorn first walked into The Stitchin' Post twenty-four years ago, after retiring from teaching and moving to Sisters, Oregon. It soon became her favorite shop, she made her first quilt, and she and shop owner Jean Wells became fast friends. Their daughters Mindi and Valori grew up wearing the one-of-a-kind garments that their mothers created.

Over the years, Lawry has been Jean's right-hand person in the business. As a quilting teacher, she developed a strong following of her own—her "mystery" classes fill before the brochure is even off the presses. Lawry has been designing quilts for the store for years, and many of her designs appear in *Four Seasons in Flannel.*

Jean Wells has been quilting for thirty-two years and is well known around the world as an author and speaker. She opened The Stitchin' Post—one of the first quilt shops in America—twenty-seven years ago. The shop shares the spotlight as one of the first shops to be featured in *American Patchwork & Quilting's* "Quilt Sampler." Jean enjoys all styles of quilting and loves to share ideas with others. Through the years, she has received many quilting and business awards, designed fabric, and been a frequent guest on HGTV's *Simply Quilts.* She and her daughter, Valori, have coauthored several quilting books with a garden theme.